Dr Sebastian Heinz

Public Enemy № 1 – Innovation

PUBLIC ENEMY № 1

INNOVATION

On the hurdles of innovation and
how to overcome them successfully.

TWIN
PRINT

Originally published in German as »Staatsfeind No. 1 – Innovation«
Transladet into English »Public Enemy No. 1 – Innovation«
Translation was done by Liam Phelan
1. Edition 2025
ISBN 978-3-96856-120-2

Publisher: Twinprint Verlag e. K., Königswinter 2025
Text: Dr Sebastian Heinz
Cover design and typesetting: Markus Werner

Printing: Libri Plureos GmbH, Friedensallee 273, 22763 Hamburg

»Everything that can go right, will go right.«

Yhprum's Law

While Murphy's Law makes us fear the worst, Yhprum's Law reminds us that life has a funny way of working out, often in ways we couldn't have planned even if we tried. It's not about blind optimism; it's about recognising that sometimes our plans falling apart leads to something unexpectedly wonderful.

HOW TO READ

It's the beginning, the first sentence that counts! With every book that captivates us. »How to read«: How do I read the book, the author, the world? You're probably reading this book for the first time; you don't know me as the author and you're wondering how this book can help you to get to know and appreciate yourself and your world better. Plenty of reasons to prepare you for reading this book. »How to read«.

»Public Enemy No. 1 – Innovation« is a collection of episodes. You can read it like a book from front to back. But you can also read it episode by episode. This allows me to provide you with a few pages of my core statements under the title of the individual episodes, which have been decisive for my path and my commitment to innovation up to this point and will remain so in the future. I would like to offer you »snackable content« and only take up your valuable time for as long as you can and want to give the topic of innovation your full attention in your everyday life. Because innovation is the most difficult part of development, it demands nothing less than our full attention!

Innovation has the advantage and the disadvantage, the opportunity and the risk that no one has done it before. That's why there is no blueprint for innovation. Despite what everyone else wants to tell you. Every innovation has its own fingerprint, its own context, its own soul. Every innovation starts with an idea that is overwhelming from the innovator's point of view. And that's a good thing. The experiences I have gathered do not claim to apply equally to all innovations. I share my experiences with you because I am convinced that there are similarities between innovations that are worth scrutinising for your own innovation based on the experiences of others. To this end, at the end of each episode I offer you key questions that you can use to apply the core messages of the episode to yourself. Understand these questions as a stimulus for your own examination of yourself, your innovation and your world and not as a checklist or blueprint for your innovation. All that matters is your innovation with its fingerprint, its context and its soul.

There are two simple reasons why my language is sometimes not so simple: Firstly, I love language and that's why I occasionally play around with it. Words and structures are my playground. Sentences, images, inner connections. It is therefore worthwhile not only to read the individual episodes, but also to feel the message between the lines. Secondly, I am a child of science. Those of you who have a doctorate, i.e. who have written a doctoral thesis themselves, know what I am writing about. The most important task of a doctoral thesis is to close a scientific gap. As banal as that sounds, it is difficult. Nevertheless, I do my best not to over-salt the »snackable content« of my episodes for you.

Which brings us to me, the author of this book. If you want to read and engage with this book, you need to know a few things about me, which I'll tell you now: I'm a Father Christmas, a Capricorn, and I'm currently in the prime of my life. At the zenith of my creative powers. I have the feeling that I can move mountains and am free from the arrogance of thinking or claiming to be able to do this alone. Innovation only succeeds with the right companions. One particular advantage that I was born with, is my twin brother. So I have never been on my own. Even in our childhood, it was never about who was better at something than the other. We were always driven by the question of what we could do better if we combined our strengths. We are also very lucky to have found a stable and happy environment in our families and to have been able to be the foundation of this ourselves. My family is an enormously important anchor of my endeavours and a supporter of my inexhaustible drive for innovation. And I have found companions with outstanding skills who make irreplaceable contributions to our joint success.

Interaction with people and the environment follows specific rules, like a game. The rules of a game have their own inner appeal for me. If I know the rules of a game, I have a real chance of winning the game – if I decide to play it at all. If, on the other hand, I don't know the rules of a game, winning is reduced to a matter of pure luck. This is something I deeply dislike, because I am many things, but by no means a gambler. The acquisition of partners and supporters for an innovation is decided according to precisely these rules. Manipulation would be the abuse of these rules for one-sided advantage. A method that, in my view, cannot be the basis for lasting success.

As a geographer specialising in development aid, I joined Deutsche Telekom's in-house consulting department after successfully passing an assessment centre and being refer-red by my father-in-law. At the end of the assessment centre, my first boss commented, with a wry smile, that he would be delighted if I brought my development aid skills to Deutsche Telekom. For me, the subsequent 16 years at Deutsche Telekom in various functions and responsibilities are and were proof that reinventing yourself doesn't just happen once, but again and again, even if you don't yet know where your journey will take you. All you need is a clear inner compass.

In order to better understand the language of the business people around me, I completed a full degree in business administration alsongside my work, which gave me the opportunity to do a doctorate. The work is called »Markterschließung im Kooperationsmodell« (Market Development in the Co-operation Model) and you can download it free of charge from the University of Duisburg-Essen website.

My dissertation presented me with a very unique challenge. As a practitioner and salesperson, I was so convinced of my idea and its genius that I simply ignored two essential points for achieving a doctorate: The requirements for scientific language and the identification and closure of a scientific gap. The feedback from my esteemed doctoral supervisor was short and concise, but enormous in its consequence: »Please use far fewer adjectives and add a little more theory.« The only sensible solution for me was to delete the entire thesis and start from scratch. In hindsight, I am extremely grateful for this journey. Nevertheless, the decision was like a painful turning point for me and was linked to the question of why I was actually making this effort. When I realised that I was only doing this for myself, to prove to myself that I fulfilled the requirements for a dissertation and therefore deserved the doctorate, all inner resistance was overcome, and the path was clear for this journey.

And that brings us to my inner drive: I am inspired by the idea that cooperation is the central prerequisite for the realisation of innovation. For me, cooperation is the antithesis of fantasies of omnipotence. Think Big is the basis of fantasies of omnipotence. And as paradoxical as it sounds: Think Bigger is the basis of cooperation. Genuine cooperation focuses on the well-being of all those involved, avoids one-sided optimisation and pools the strengths of the individual partners. In game theory, we call such constellations »coalitions« and the individual players »coalition members«. Where the journey ends ingloriously can be observed regularly when coalitions, for example in politics, break down or fail to achieve their own goals. First the common goal erodes, then the co-operation, then the communication with and about each other and finally the whole plan. However, if you strive for genuine cooperation from the outset and in all consistency, as a pleasant side effect you exclude those who have their own self-optimisation in mind first and foremost and enjoy the benefit of companions who help you to actually bring innovation into the world. This requires reading the world. The context, the people, the environment.

Why am I writing this book right now? How did I come to the crazy conclusion that my experiences could be even in the slightest use for you and your innovation? For over 12 years, I have been working on a genuine innovation in a key industry with social, even global relevance: A fundamentally new battery. Batteries are an elementary component of the global mobility and energy transition. We have named our solution to the challenges of battery ageing the »HPB Solid-State Battery«. Prof Dr Günther Hambitzer, the inventor of this technology, has invested almost his entire scientific career and much of his private life in this innovation. I myself was able to accompany him in various roles and functions. This has not only resulted in a deep friendship. I can look back on 12 years of experience in a shark tank of innovation, 12 years of »all-in«, 12 years of consistency and 12 years of successfully fighting for survival. A time in which we asked all the questions of entrepreneurship again and again and turned the answers upside down again and again. Always with the indomitable will to successfully bring this innovation to market – not to get fabulously rich, but because technologies of this calibre are of crucial importance for the development of society as a whole. I have learnt that the better the innovation, the greater the resistance to it. This is because you step on the toes of many who capitalise on the »*status quo*« and for whom change means danger. The fact that we still exist despite everything, even though the stars are sometimes falling faster than they are rising, especially in the battery sector, fills me with pride. These 12 years have taken incredible energy, connected countless people and provided a cornucopia of experiences that could be of importance to you.

If my episodes provide relevant inspiration for you, I will have achieved my goal. And if just one of you finds the path to success for your innovation as a result, this book will have been more than worthwhile. Because I believe that innovators across the board face similar challenges. Successful innovations often serve as role models. People tend to be reluctant to talk about the stumbling blocks. However, these obstacles are often not rooted in the innovation itself, but rather in the environment and how you deal with them. And this is exactly what you have in your own hands if you manage to read your world.

Enough preamble and good luck with your innovation!

»HOW TO READ«

- › Do I know myself?
- › Who am I?
- › Where do I come from?
- › What characterises me as a person and personality?
- › What is important to me?
- › How do I deal with difficulties?
- › What drives me?

Contents

CLIMATE CHANGE AND OTHER DIVISIVE ISSUES

What's inside

Climate change is one of the most controversial issues in the world. It divides societies in many places. Instead of translating the pressure to act into a new vision for the world, prosperity and climate change are being played off against each other. As if one existed without the consequences of the other. This discussion completely overshadows the power of innovation and the enormous boost to prosperity that a pioneering role in scalable, technological solutions can bring. However, »climate change« can also be synonymous with »the threat of something new«. This episode looks at why we don't need climate change to justify the rationale behind the energy and mobility transition and why it is still so difficult to do the right thing.

The episode

Fossil fuels such as lignite, hard coal, crude oil and natural gas are essentially no different from renewable energy sources such as wind power, solar energy, hydropower or biomass. A significant and indeed considerable difference lies in the rate of formation, i.e. the time required to form the respective energy source. The formation of fossil fuels is based on tectonic processes that lead to the formation of these energy sources over thousands of years. Renewable energy sources, on the other hand, are available in the short term.

There are also significant differences with regard to the distribution of energy sources: due to the sheer duration of the formation of fossil energy sources and their tectonic formation processes, the deposits are permanent and »*a priori*« fixed for our use. The distribution does not change geographically in our time, but in proportion to the discovery of new deposits, technical progress and the value of the raw material. The higher the demand, the more profitable the exploitation, and the better the technology, the more efficient its extraction and utilisation. The distribution of renewable energies is also determined »*a priori*«, but in terms of their generation they are available at much shorter notice and their exploitation, at least in the case of wind, solar and biomass, is essentially dependent on the use of technology, not on a geological deposit.

However, renewable energies also have a disadvantage, a disadvantage that is repeatedly cited when it comes to the battle between fossil fuels and renewable energies: their volatility, i.e. their dependence on local climatic events. On the other hand, the technical utilisation of fossil fuels is very controllable. A secure power supply depends on the ability of energy suppliers to cover energy requirements at all times. The more volatile and therefore erratic the availability of an energy source, the more difficult it is to balance generation and consumption. Does this mean that the decision has already been made in favour of fossil fuels? Apparently yes and certainly no.

An example of the greater complexity of reality: hydropower is naturally dependent on the distribution of rivers, reservoirs and bodies of water and therefore on the regional topology and climatic conditions of the region. Climate change poses a particular threat to this energy source because the availability of hydropower on the mainland – and therefore also the cooling capacity for nuclear power plants – depends on precipitation events. Periods of prolonged drought make this energy source unpredictably volatile – even extremely dangerous in the absence of reactor cooling. Nuclear power is therefore indirectly »on a drip« from hydropower.

In geopolitical terms, there are three main causes of conflict: energy, food and water. On the positive side, it is about security of supply; on the negative side, it is about distribution disputes. A lack of security of supply is the cause of wars and global refugee flows. The dependence of energy supply on fossil and nuclear energy sources harbours considerable risks for all those countries that do not have sufficient reserves or geological deposits of their own. For this simple geopolitical reason alone, it would generally be more advantageous than disadvantageous to base one's own energy supply on energy sources that are under one's own control. Although wind power, solar energy, biomass and hydropower are volatile, in the event of a conflict they cannot be switched off from outside without considerable effort and a forced energy crisis cannot be used as a tactical weapon. The war in Ukraine has also clearly shown that the security of food supplies, especially the concentration of global wheat stocks in just a few countries, can have a global impact on forced famines and thus refugee flows. Access to water, and in particular, to clean drinking water, is the third relevant reason for war, especially as this resource becomes increasingly scarce due to growing drought. This scarcity also has implications for the security of food and energy supply.

A completely different dimension opens up when you consider everything that can be produced from fossil raw materials. Crude oil in particular is the basis for many products, from plastics to important medical products. Many of these products can be converted into new products through recycling, so that the raw material can be used several times. This does not yet take into account the innovations we will see based on these raw materials. However, when used as an energy source, whether for power generation, heat generation or mobility, it is utilised through combustion. Subsequent utilisation is therefore ruled out. Quite apart from the release of CO_2 bound over the ages and the associated consequences for climate change. Burning is therefore certainly the most stupid utilisation for these special raw materials.

As long as extraction is faster than formation, the sources of these raw materials will dry up sooner or later in purely mathematical terms. The responsibility for a more intelligent use of resources lies in our hands. A »fire and forget« mentality or the excuse that there is nothing more we can do in the few years until we retire is inexcusable towards our children and grandchildren.

These findings are not new. Nor do they require extensive prior knowledge. They are not even particularly complicated, and yet we are witnessing a battle between the supposed opponents of prosperity and climate change. The reason for this lies in the personal sensitivities and egoisms in which we are all caught up. The transformation of the energy supply towards renewable energies will take decades and cannot be completed in one legislative period. It requires investment in generation technologies, but above all in storage technologies. It requires a rethink, a new vision for the future, new ways of achieving security of supply – at the end of the day, a veritable El Dorado for innovation! It is important that we do not play the individual innovations off against each other, but instead discuss how all these innovations can complement each other to enable a better future.

At this point, I would like to give you three examples of the fight for innovation that I find very impressive: Over 100 years ago, Rudolf Diesel invented the diesel engine. It was an invention that nobody wanted at the time and yet it became the basis of an unprecedented industrial revolution. Rudolf Diesel received nothing from his invention and died impoverished. In 2007, the first iPhone was launched in Germany exclusively by T-Mobile, the mobile phone subsidiary of Deutsche Telekom. At the time, I was working in sales strategy at Deutsche Telekom. Nobody in sales wanted to sell iPhones. The mobile device trend was all about miniaturisation, large screens were seen as a step backwards and there was no sign of cameras or apps. Nokia, Blackberry, Motorola and Sony Ericsson were the undisputed top dogs. It was only when the target of 1 million mobile devices at the end of 2007 was enforced by the then Chief Sales Officer that the iPhone's triumphal march in Germany began. All the conveniences that we take for granted today were unimaginable for most people at the time. It was the vision of Steve Jobs, the founder of Apple, the vision of an impressive innovator.

There are certainly several examples of this. I find these two particularly impressive because they have taken on a special significance recently: Since the passionate debate about the sense and nonsense of electromobility, the diesel engine has enjoyed a recognition that it never had at the time of its invention and had to fight hard for over time against all odds. The countless amenities and conveniences associated with today's smartphones were unthinkable just a few years ago. They originated in the minds of a few innovators who were not satisfied with the »*status quo*« and consistently pursued their path against all odds. With hindsight, it is very easy to say: »It was clear that this innovation would prevail.« But it wasn't. Many people say: »We should have invested back then, then we would be fabulously rich today.« The problem with this is that the decision in favour of innovation is not made in hindsight, but well before turning onto the winning road.

I would therefore like to take you to the point where the course has not yet been set and the decision has not yet been made with the third example: the discovery of the HPB Solid-State Battery. The innovation that I have been fighting for consistently for 12 years now and have done everything I can to achieve. For more than thirty years, our inventor, Prof Dr Günther Hambitzer, has been driven by the question of how to solve battery ageing at its chemical root. And he has answered this question with a completely new battery system. He has the ability to see the chemical processes in his mind's eye. As an avowed fan of the brain as the greatest gift to us humans, I truly bow down to this intellectual achievement.

We know today that there is no alternative to the energy and mobility transition for many reasons. We also know that this requires enormous investment in storage technologies and that the technologies available today are not yet at the level we need in order not to solve one sustainability problem with another. Battery storage systems have a special role to play here for short-term storage. Reason enough to combine the issues of sustainability, safety and longevity? No. For many, this is not sufficient motivation. Rather, the aim is to maintain the »*status quo*« for as long as possible. With the already noticeable consequence that we are being left further and further behind by nations that are fundamentally more open to innovation in this area. Instead of giving innovators the space and resources they need to create »the next big thing«, innovations are being played off against each other and placed in opposition to securing prosperity. Many other nations are miles ahead of us in this respect.

Our, my journey to this point is what I mean by the fight for innovation. It encompasses the entire duration, from idea to realisation, with all the adversity that entails, before everyone says: »I've always said that your solution is urgently needed!« This battle is a battle with highs and lows, a permanent alternation of hot and cold, always unpredictable. A battle that requires you to scrutinise yourself every day and reinvent yourself if necessary – without losing sight of your innovation and its potential.

What it's all about

»Climate change« is synonymous with »the threat of something new«. No matter how controversial the debates surrounding your innovation are, there is a good reason for your idea. Your hard lot: innovators only get the credit when most of the risks have been cleared out of the way and the first millions have been earned. But before that, it's important to believe in the innovation and fight for it. Many debates can be resolved by turning the opposition between innovation A and innovation B into a coexistence. If you seek to complement each other.

A good example from the field of storage technologies is the »marriage of storage technologies«, the combination of hydrogen and batteries, instead of playing off the two technologies against each other in favour of maintaining a »*status quo*« that is at least questionable. The contrast: If we wanted to realise individual mobility with hydrogen instead of battery storage, we would need 2.5 times the gross energy production for the same mileage due to the poorer energy efficiency of hydrogen compared to a traction battery. The great advantage of hydrogen production is that the necessary electrolysers can use any energy for hydrogen production. This means that almost any amount of surplus electricity can be used for hydrogen production. The addition: However, electrolysers are at their optimum in a partial load range, i.e. not at minimum and not at maximum load. The electricity production of wind turbines is so high that the storage of excess energy in batteries alone is not suitable for achieving maximum yield. The marriage: The combination of wind power, hydrogen production and battery storage would make it possible to run the electrolysers at their operating optimum for longer with the surplus electricity from wind power and thus harvest more net electricity generation than with the current standard shutdown. The sequel: the hydrogen could ultimately be used to produce green steel, and the battery storage units could be used to smooth out the feed-in power. So, let's move away from opposites and towards complementarity. Simply »more net from gross« of the generation capacities already installed. Fundamental positions produce fundamental oppositions. Fundamental opposition produces standstill. Standstill prevents progress and jeopardises prosperity. This is the connection that needs to be broken.

Whatever your innovation is, take care to build bridges. Bridges to other innovators. Build an ecosystem of partners and supporters. This turns the battle of innovations into a space of options for a better future. A better future through the use and combination of many innovations. Then it's easier – and more fun, too.

How to read

»CLIMATE CHANGE AND OTHER DIVISIVE ISSUES«

› In what context does my innovation take place?

› Where are the supposed lines of conflict with the »*status quo*« and other innovations?

› What do they have in common?

› How can you help each other?

› How do I tell the story as an invitation to join in?

› How do I become a bridge builder to other innovations?

› What keeps me enjoying my innovation?

THINK BIG – THINK BIGGER

What's inside:

»Think Big« is the appeal of all investors when it comes to increasing the attractiveness of an innovation for outsiders and making the innovation »tasty« for investors. »Think big« focuses on differentiation and competitive advantages, scalability and dominance. This appeal always includes setting oneself apart from others in order to secure one's own advantages in the long term, and thus maximise capitalisation for oneself and investors. Once learned, never forgotten: you can't teach an old dog new tricks. This episode looks at why this appeal can lead in the wrong direction and regularly forms a fine line between fantasies of omnipotence and actual success, why this appeal can dilute the actual innovation and what a powerful alternative genuine collaborations offer.

The episode

Innovation fires the imagination. What would be possible and achievable if only everyone recognised the same advantages in an innovation that the innovator has so clearly in mind with his innovation? It is only in an initial, often fleeting moment that the focus is on the actual core of the innovation; on what makes the innovation special and which problems it solves better or perhaps even for the first time. Thoughts very quickly wander and the enormous radiance of the almost incomprehensible financial opportunities of global market success appear before the mind's eye. An almost magical attraction arises. The idea begins to inspire others.

If you look directly into the sun, you are quickly dazzled. Depending on the intensity, a »blind spot« remains in the field of vision, which usually disappears sooner or later. The radiance of the possible, immeasurable wealth of innovations has the same effect on the depth of innovation. It causes the focus to shift to the personal or investor-side economic benefits, thereby overshadowing relevant issues outside of this radiance, which can, however, be no less critical to success.

Technological innovations with a high degree of complexity are particularly affected by this. Many innovations are also affected by the fact that specialised knowledge is required to implement the idea. »Doing your homework« is what matters now.

Jeff Bezos' idea was extremely simple. He had the idea of setting up an online bookshop through which he also wanted to sell fridges. When he presented this idea to the board of Bertelsmann, the top dog for book clubs in Germany at the time, he was literally laughed at and summarily thrown out. Thomas Middelhoff, who was at Bertelsmann at the time and a participant in this meeting, once categorised this process as follows: With the knowledge we have today, every participant in this memorable board meeting would like to be so flexible that they could bite themselves in their ass every day for this narrow-minded rejection of this idea.

As simple as Jeff Bezos' idea was, the risk of sharing it with someone who could be useful to him for his own realisation, but who could also potentially have stolen the idea due to a relatively low barrier. At this point, however, the idea was just an idea. There was no evidence that this idea had any chance of success. Jeff Bezos was just one of those American storytellers who probably wanted to get rich quick by taking a top dog on board.

The harsh rejection from Bertelsmann has not deterred Jeff Bezos from realising his idea. With his company Amazon, he has quickly become one of the richest people in the world. And that is precisely what makes him a shining example for many innovators and investors. He stuck to his innovation and realised it himself – against all odds. James Dyson can look back on a similar story. His innovation, a hoover without a bag, was rejected by the top dogs. That's why he realised it himself – with groundbreaking success.

So where is the blind spot in these two examples, where is the fork in the road where there is a risk of taking a wrong turn? To stay in the picture: If you look at the stories of Jeff Bezos, James Dyson and other exceptional entrepreneurs from the point of view of the result, from the point of view of their present-day radiance, it seems as if these entrepreneurs had managed it all on their own, as if they were omnipotent in their creative endeavours, as if they had foreseen it all. We lose sight of the fact that these stories were confronted with the rejection of their time, which – without the unconditional will to realise their innovators' ideas – would have meant the end of innovation. The initial impetus for realising the ideas of Jeff Bezos and James Dyson was the supposedly easy route via the top dogs in their respective industries. And in doing so, they had to overcome nothing less than the top dogs' internal rejection of innovation from outside. The more established an industry and the bigger the top dogs, the more resounding the laughter in the faces of the innovators. No established car manufacturer believed that Elon Musk would be able to profitably enter the mass production of cars. Today, this has been copied several times by various Asian manufacturers such as BYD and has resulted in a serious management error on the executive floors of the formerly undisputed top dogs.

A look behind the scenes invites us to review our perspective. If we look at the charisma of Amazon and the incredible success of Jeff Bezos, it turns out that from the very beginning, it was not about realising the underlying innovation of »books and fridges« alone. Rather, from the very beginning, there was an interest in working with partners to achieve faster realisation and faster growth. The fallacy of the blind spot when considering Amazon's attractiveness – and such examples serve as the basis for the »Think Big« appeal – lies in the fact that the path of »realisation on one's own« appears to be the only promising path. As a result, you only have to think big enough and realise everything on your own to follow the blueprint for success that Jeff Bezos, James Dyson and other innovators have presented with their successes. An omnipotence fantasy that many innovators fail miserably at.

It's the opposite that counts. The homework must be done.

It helps to be aware of your own limitations and to consistently look for cooperation. Things that you cannot or cannot yet do yourself can be contributed by others. However, it is essential not to indulge in your own fantasy of omnipotence and degrade others to mere fulfilment assistants. It is important to effectively invite others to co-operate, support and partner with you. This requires nothing less than the ability to connect people and build genuine cooperation. Genuine co-operations differ from non-genuine collaborations in that they are designed to be mutually beneficial in the long term. Non-genuine collaborations are, for example, pure service contracts for the fulfilment of which a previously agreed price is paid. However, if I expect partners to support my innovation, perhaps even to take a risk, I have to offer them a »piece of the pie« on the other side. This doesn't always have to be shares. It's more about creating a »permanent risk and profit-sharing community« in which each partner receives an attractive and fair share of the success in the long term compared to the risk they take on. Genuine co-operations have the charm of being able to reduce investment costs, because issues that the innovator cannot, or cannot yet do themselves can be provided by partners who have the necessary experience and resources. Co-operations also have the opportunity to combine the strengths of different players far more effectively than would ever be possible by building up all the skills and resources in-house.

»Think Big« can be the gateway to the failure of innovation due to the risk of omnipotence fantasies. Building genuine co-operations in order to do the necessary homework opens up additional resources and allows you to think bigger than your own resource situation allows. »Think Bigger« is the guideline that an innovation, and with it the innovator, can follow from the idea to its realisation in order to increase their own chances of success and not fail miserably at »Think Big«. »Do it yourself« is then the last resort, the final option in the event that there are not enough co-operation partners available, but not the blueprint from the start of the journey.

What it's all about

»Think Big« is both an invitation and a challenge to learn from successful innovators and to adapt, if not copy, their strategies for your own success. The challenge lies in the fact that the focus on growth and size can obscure the view of what homework can realistically be done in what time frame and what risks are associated with rapid scaling of innovation. Investors who issue this slogan often demand that innovators set themselves »ambitious goals«, clearly state what resources they need to achieve them in the short term, only to realise at the end of this relatively short period – which often only lasts a year – that this plan has not worked. The result is the need for another round of financing, for which new investors once again issue the slogan »Think Big«. The loop of »ambitious goals« starts all over again. In the world of finance, these loops are called »rounds«. They are not numbered but sorted alphabetically: A-B-C-D rounds. The plot of »Think Big« gets bigger with each round, the cake gets bigger and bigger through dilution, until the actual innovator is just a side note to the innovation. As the innovator shrinks, so does the motivation for success. Failure becomes the rule. In the end, the only thing that often counts is whether you got off lightly or bounced back in time with a tidy profit. By then, the actual innovation has long since become irrelevant. The fantasy of omnipotence is followed by failure and the bigger the fantasy of omnipotence, the bigger the bang at the end of the story.

This can currently be seen impressively in the battery sector. Many innovators are making grandiose announcements about their technological superiority and their ambitious plans. But very few do their homework. The big money is too tempting and the time pressure seems too great. These stories have been a real goldmine for investors for several years. The stories got bigger and bigger, the announcements more and more gigantic. Even far beyond the point of reality and meaningfulness. In return, essential »details« were repeatedly omitted that would have enabled the layman to see through the deceptive packaging.

One of my absolute lowlights was delivered by Toyota, for example: »1,200 km range in 10 minutes on a charge« was one of those completely exaggerated announcements that travelled through the press like a tsunami. Checked by our critical journalists? Not a chance. If you add 15 kWh/100 km to the missing »detail« of consumption, for example, the simple rule of three results in a charging quantity of 180 kWh for a range of 1,200 km, which can only be transferred in 10 minutes with a charging power of 1,080 kW. Technical and heat losses are not even taken into account. The maximum charging speed of 350 kW at fast charging stations would therefore require the use of three charging cables in parallel, which would still leave 30 kW of charging power missing. We haven't even talked about the required battery size of at least 180 kWh – again without any realistic allowance due to the chemicals used and their efficiencies and restrictions –

compared to the average 75 kWh used today. What a load of rubbish!

The success story of Northvolt, which I personally have always wanted to see succeed, ended with a bankruptcy for which the state of Schleswig-Holstein and the federal government can be held liable due to a guarantee totalling €600 million. Investors in the earlier rounds have pocketed the profits, while the taxpayer bears a painful part of the considerable risks of the omnipotence fantasy.

These examples of »think big« represent an enormous barrier to entry for innovators who do their homework first in two respects: On the one hand, innovators are being asked to do it like Northvolt or Freyr by potential investors. On the other hand, the failure of these models is taken as justification for not entering the market until the next time. Experience has shown that the risks are far too great.

Surviving in this environment requires genuine cooperation and supporters who help to systematically complete the homework to an extent and at a speed that the respective resources allow. Fantasies of omnipotence are absolutely out of place here. »Think Bigger« through cooperation, on the other hand, is essential, even necessary for survival.

How to read

»THINK BIG – THINK BIGGER«

› Where do I currently stand with my innovation?

› What homework do I still have to do – regardless of the possible scaling?

› What skills do I have to achieve my goals?

› What skills do I lack?

› What can I offer genuine co-operation partners in order to establish a stable risk and profit-sharing community with them?

› How can I recognise that I am about to fall into the trap of the omnipotence fantasy from »Think Big«?

› »Think Bigger«: How much more can I achieve if I think in terms of real cooperation?

THERE IS A MAGIC IN EVERY BEGINNING

What's inside

The idea for innovation, the first steps along the way, the design, the founding of the company, the first companions – all of this has a magic all of its own. There are no limits, there is only boundless freedom of thought, the vastness of your own imagination. Everything is positive. Everything is geared towards success. Thoughts of failure do not want to arise, and if they do, they are stifled in the most positive sense by the euphoria of the beginning. And that's a good thing. On the other hand, the statistics speak against this happiness. Too many innovations fail and the road becomes unexpectedly hard and rocky relatively quickly. This makes it all the more important, especially at the beginning, to take a look beyond the horizon and – as paradoxical as it sounds – to think about the possibility of failure in a positive mood. That's what this episode is all about.

The episode

There is a widespread myth: everyone is equal. This is true before the law and before God. This is not true when it comes to founding a company and the start of innovation and, in particular, its development. Despite all the joy and unity at the time of founding, there is always one important player missing: the future.

I don't know of any start-up project that has already received sufficient funding for the entire journey. This does not mean that there are not some lucky projects that have benefited from complete and sufficient financing for the entire project. This aspect of innovation has a particular impact on start-ups. As a rule, the »future-drunk« founders – and this is meant exclusively in a positive sense – sit at the notary's office and divide the company equally among themselves as a matter of course. Only the future is left empty-handed. All problems are shifted to the future, complexity has no place at this moment. On the contrary: if they did not divide the company equally among themselves, there would be an imbalance between the founders. The antithesis of equality and the peace that comes with it. The distribution of shares is thus stylised into a problem of appreciation, although there are good reasons to solve the distribution differently.

Assuming that the founders cannot provide sufficient funds for the journey to realisation, sooner or later the question arises as to where fresh capital should come from. There are then two basic strategies: on the one hand, the cake can be enlarged in order to give new shareholders a fresh slice of the cake. This is also known as dilution. On the other hand, one or more of the founders can give up some of their shares in order to finance the company. And this is precisely where the risk lies. Once you have shares, you are extremely reluctant to give them back. No matter how natural it is for you at the time of founding. It then depends on the distribution of voting shares whether and in what form the founding team can solve the challenge of the upcoming financing. Every transfer of shares, every dilution hurts, as if something is being taken away. At this moment, fears of loss and egoism come to the fore that were unthinkable in the euphoria of the beginning and are also completely authentically absent. Blocking out the future is therefore a significant realisation risk that is inherent in innovation right from the start.

We chose a different path for the realisation of our innovation. A path that was based on a clear principle that still applies today: without the innovative achievement of our inventor, none of us would have the chance to be part of this innovation. Perhaps it is also due to the impression of a hostile takeover that our inventor had to go through, which was associated with every conceivable existential fear. In any case, we were adamant that he should be the majority shareholder by a clear margin – both at the time the company was founded and along the way. At the same time, we jointly decided that each wave of financing should be funded for as long as possible by gradually transferring our inventor's shares to the company's own holdings. For the co-founders and all other shareholders, this arrangement has the extremely positive effect of ensuring that their shares are not diluted. Conversely, our inventor can rely on the fact that a hostile takeover can no longer occur, as this would always require a majority resolution, which he himself can prevent thanks to the absolute majority he has secured.

Of course, this model did not mean that all the co-founders of the early phase shared this idea from the outset. Nor was our model completely free of any discussions about distribution. Nevertheless, this model has given us a clear focus on realisation for years, because nobody has to take the risk of losing anything: The inventor does not lose the company through a hostile takeover, the co-partners do not lose their shares in the company.

During the further development of the company, we realised that the admission of new shareholders to a German GmbH is at least costly due to the notary requirement. In addition, the smallest denomination of shares is limited to one euro. With a share capital of € 25,000, you therefore have a maximum of 25,000 shares unless you systematically increase the liable equity capital, which in turn corresponds to a dilution that we did not want. We were lucky that one of our founding partners had a Swiss AG that he was able to bring into our company. Here, the liable equity capital must be at least CHF 100,000, but the denomination of the shares is possible down to CHF 0.01. This corresponds to 10 million shares instead of 25,000 GmbH shares. We have made the Swiss AG the 100 % parent company of the German GmbH through a reverse merger with equal shares. We have set up the AG as a pure holding company, while the German GmbH continues to bundle the operating business. This has given us the opportunity to turn many supporters into shareholders. We now have over 300, and all of this without any dilution at a price per share that increases as we progress. Because we always sell from the company's own stock, the new shareholders' investment flows directly into the company. A structure that is advantageous for everyone involved, and one that I am truly proud of.

What it's all about

Despite all the euphoria of the foundation, it's important not to systematically exclude the most important player at the table: The future. It's worth realising your goals, wishes, dreams, fears and risks and having transparent conversations with your co-founders. It is important to allow the thought that there will very likely be a need for further funding in the future. It is worthwhile for everyone involved to think ahead about this without failing to realise it due to individual and deep-seated fears and risks. There is no blueprint for this. It's about your innovation. It has its own fingerprint, its own character, its own soul. It's about inviting the future to the founding table and giving it and its design the space it deserves. This provides security, stability and the necessary focus on the path to realisation.

How to read

»THERE IS A MAGIC IN EVERY BEGINNING«

› What is the special magic of my innovation?

› Who would I like to have on my founding team and why?

› Do I know my goals, wishes, dreams, fears and risks – and those of my co-founders and companions?

› Have I reserved a chair for the future in the circle of founders? If not, how do we make up for it together?

› How do we celebrate the foundation and our joint successes?

› How do we support each other when there is stress, and what rules should apply when we live apart?

› What is our recipe for a satisfied »innovation flat share»?

WITH WATER WINGS ON THE HIGH SEAS

What's inside

Stress is an unavoidable ingredient in any innovation. Not everything goes according to plan, not everything works out. On the contrary: sooner or later there will be a creak in the woodwork, there will be arguments, there will be a bang. In the worst case, the very existence of the company and thus the survival of the innovation is suddenly at stake. This is the moment when your own DNA comes into play. Your own inner attitude – to stress, to failure, to the death of your own innovation. To your own attitude towards your environment. It is the moment when, due to different stress tolerances at different times, you, your co-founders and your companions are in danger of drowning. It is the moment that decides the future as well as the foundation. The inner attitude makes the difference. That's what this episode is about.

The episode

It is difficult to convey how it feels when your own innovation is on the brink of extinction. When it threatens to die. It is equally difficult to imagine what it is like when you are actually drowning. Nevertheless, the analogy between the two extreme situations seems to me to be a suitable way of describing what is important, namely to put your inner attitude to the test in a way that can only be achieved in comparison with an extreme situation.

I imagine that I have been floating on the high seas for so long, without protection or help, and only supported by two water wings that have weakend under the harsh sun. The water wings fail and I realise that I only have enough strength for half an hour at most before I drown. But then suddenly a rubber dinghy appears. New, gleaming, steered by a skipper who offers to save me. But before the joy and gratitude of being rescued can take my breath away and make me forget about swimming for a moment, the skipper presents me with the conditions under which he wants to rescue me. It is at that moment I realise that I would never have accepted these conditions if I had been on land – i.e. in safety. But now I'm in a different situation: I only have the strength for half an hour. I'm on the brink of drowning. What would you decide? Would you accept the conditions and allow yourself to be rescued?

Before I give you my answer to this question, I would like to transfer you to the company situation. There is a moment on the way to realising an innovation when the financial resources run out. This is the moment when it is a matter of life and death for the company. Of course, there are different options for the continuation of an innovation –

even after the death of a company. But I am concerned with another, decisive point. Let's call our skipper Mr Meyer. That's a synonym for a lot of people, because the name is very common. And that's what matters. So Mr Meyer appears on the scene at a time when the company is in a critical situation. He senses this and offers an investment that provides real financial relief. However, he presents an offer in which it is clear from the outset that he wants to be granted such special rights that it is virtually impossible for other investors to come on board. It is precisely this stalemate situation that you cannot prepare for – neither yourself, nor the others, nor each other. It is the situation in which you have to make a decision in favour of the threat of a quick death or the certainty of a creeping death. This is the moment when your inner attitude matters.

Back to my decision-making situation on the high seas: in my imagination, I bite into the skipper's fantastic inflatable boat, push off with my last ounce of strength and go under laughing. Why? I know that I have to die at some point. But I also know that this skipper will never forget my laughter for the rest of his life. I make this decision in the full knowledge that I will die. But I am also making this decision in the full knowledge that I would never have accepted these conditions on land – in a safe environment. So, I say to Mr Meyer with all due sincerity: "Please fuck off!"

The rationale behind this decision is very simple, even though the consequence of this decision is anything but simple: The moment I would accept the terms of the rescue, I would immediately find myself in safety. At the same moment, I would deeply regret the decision, because in the burgeoning peace of security I would realise that I had chosen certain death in instalments. This decision can no longer be reversed in an entrepreneurial context.

Specifically, this involves preference shares, special voting rights, decision-making powers, veto rights, liquidation preferences and much more, which usually results in a one-sided exploitation of the innovator. An overreach that no other investor would accept, but would possibly also demand for themselves. These are negotiating positions »on land«, completely detached from the existential threat of broken wings on the high seas. These are negotiating positions that make it clear that Mr Meyer simply does not care whether you accept these conditions, or another desperate innovator agrees to them. These Mr Meyers are not interested in innovation at all. It's about playing on the innovator's existential fear and the thrill of successfully negotiating the most outrageous possible demand. The fun of exploring the outer limits of the innovator's capacity for suffering. Mr Meyer does not strengthen you and your innovation; he weakens you and tries to put himself in a particularly good position in case you fail. On the way there, Mr Meyer will make further demands that you would accept again because you have already made the first decision. That is unfair and insincere. It is no more appropriate than taking a hostage or blackmailing someone – and yet it happens all too often.

What it's all about

You are in control of your own destiny at all times. There is not a single threat to your innovation that could force you to accept conditions that, if considered reasonably, will not only be nonsensical but even dangerous for your innovation.

The only way you can find out if the skipper means well is

to maximise transparency. Transparency is a powerful tool: it is the foundation for all those who mean business and a sharp sword against all those who have something to hide. Tell them openly and clearly why the conditions they are demanding of you are unacceptable. Explain this neutrally and in relation to the goal of your innovation. If possible, offer them alternatives that are feasible for you in the long term and that feel good. The more he insists on his positions, which you have made clear to him that and why they are detrimental to you and the implementation of your innovation and therefore unacceptable to you, the clearer it becomes that the skipper is a Mr Meyer. Then protect yourself and your innovation through consistency and attitude – and send Mr Meyer packing.

How to read

»WITH WATER WINGS ON THE HIGH SEAS«

› What values and convictions drive me?

› What is irrevocable for me in my dealings?

› Am I prepared to go to extremes?

› Am I prepared to accept that the path of my innovation can also fail, but then not in complete self-loathing?

› Why should I accept conditions that I would never accept under normal circumstances – what would be better or worse as a result?

› Who are my Mr Meyers? Where did I meet them, and what did I learn from the encounters?

› What do I gain by giving Mr Meyer the boot?

PACTA SUNT SERVANDA

What's inside

If I was interested in paragraphs, I would have studied law. This is a widespread opinion among non-lawyers. And therefore also a widespread opinion among founders and innovators. Loosely translated, »pacta sunt servanda« means that contracts must be honoured. An elementary principle that we have inherited from the Romans. The challenge is that the contract is at the beginning of a collaboration, but the legal dispute is only at the end. The regular time lag between the conclusion of the contract and the legal dispute obscures the enormous relevance of good contracts for many innovators. This episode looks at what good contracts are and why it is not just the terms and conditions that is important.

The episode

Synergy takes centre stage at the beginning of a collaboration. The contracting parties realise that they can achieve something together that each of them could not achieve alone. The mood is positive and everyone is looking forward to working together. Given the congruence of the goals and visions, there is no sign that there could be a dispute. It's downright distracting during the discussions.

Many of us are overwhelmed by contract texts and legalese. The language is often unwieldy, the regulations too detailed. The connections are difficult to recognise. We prefer to concentrate on the »big picture«. After all, it has to be right if we want to reach our goal together.

Focusing on the »big picture« can indeed work for a long time. However, it ends abruptly the moment one of the contracting parties thinks it has been taken advantage of by another contracting party. Then an accusation arises. The accusation that the other party has not kept to the agreements. But which agreements should the party have adhered to? When it comes down to it, only the contractual agreements count. In other words, exactly what is set out in contracts – whether written or verbal. With contractual texts, every word, every formulation, every exception, every restriction, every obligation and every right suddenly matters. Every little detail. On the inner connections. Now you suddenly realise what you have actually agreed to. It's not uncommon for you to slap yourself in the face and wonder how this could have happened. Surely there was absolute agreement? How could it all have gone so wrong? Why are people now harping on about the details when it was actually always about the »big picture«? That's right: something like this must not happen.

Contracts can only be amended retrospectively if both parties agree. Correcting a mistake, or an imbalance, is therefore only possible as long as you are either still in the contract negotiations, or you still understand each other well and still share the »big picture«. In any case, before the first signs of conflict emerge. The earlier this course correction is made, the easier it is but the less foreseeable the conflict is. The less relevant the annoying detail in a brittle text appears. It is much easier to harmonise the common ground, the »big picture«. So how can this balancing act be overcome? What is the right recipe? And how can it be enjoyable?

This is only possible with the right motivation: yes, contracts are signed because the paperwork is somehow part of the process, and hopefully they disappear into a drawer forever. And that's exactly how it should stay. However, it is much easier to open Pandora's box in the event of a dispute and put these contracts back on the table if you know in advance exactly what you have put in the drawer. And that what you have put in the drawer is still fair and in order in the event of a dispute. Because that's the only thing that matters. A contract is completely superfluous if it works the way all parties want it to. A contract only unfolds its sometimes overwhelming relevance when the common path becomes bumpy, the paths separate or have already separated. This is when the dirty laundry is washed. A bad contract is dirty laundry. Contracts are good if the rules of the collaboration are agreed in the best spirit at the beginning and are also regulated in detail for the event that the collaboration ends, for whatever reason.

The good news for all non-lawyers: the clearer and more

comprehensible a contract is written, the better. After all, a contract is a consensual declaration of intent by the contracting parties. But how can a declaration of intent fit if I don't understand it myself? Signing a contract that I do not understand or whose consequences I do not comprehend is not a suitable reflection of my will. Because I maintain that we all know what we want. We just get scared of legalese. This fear is unfounded. If you are not comfortable with legalese, please ask your lawyer. Ask him what the clause, the sentence, the word, simply everything you don't understand means. But please also ask whether what you think you have understood will be interpreted in the same way in the event of a legal dispute.

An example from our world of licensing illustrates the importance of these questions: as technology developers and licensors, we have a strong interest in only having to disclose those things that are relevant to the conclusion of the contract during licence agreement negotiations.

Technology secrets should not be disclosed unless contractually agreed to exercise the licence and backs this up with a corresponding payment, for example. Particularly in the case of more complex innovations, there is often a discrepancy between the innovator and the interested party. The interested party regularly tries to make it clear to the innovator that without comprehensive due diligence – an inspection of the »*status quo*« – an assessment of the innovation is not possible, and a contract cannot be concluded. The preservation of business secrets is contrasted with the prospect of a lucrative agreement.

Irrespective of this disparity, every due diligence process involves effort – including on the part of the innovator. And this is where the effort really piles up, because many interested parties carry out this due diligence on an innovator. Each interested party has their own agenda, their own idea, their own questions – simply their own view of everything that concerns you and your innovation. But with all the effort involved for each interested party, it usually takes longer than expected. Over time, the need to have this effort compensated by the interested parties increases. At least that's the case for us. A very catchy and well-known concept is the so-called »break-up fee«, a payment that is due if contract negotiations are broken off. It is intended to compensate the innovator for the time and effort involved in accompanying the due diligence process, while at the same time underpinning the interest of the interested party. After all, nobody signs a penalty payment if they are not seriously interested.

And that's where the devil is in the detail: When it comes to large contracts, the amounts involved are high. A break-up fee has an effect if it is proportionate to the contract value, i.e. in particular if it is not set too low. Intuitively, 10 % does not appear to be too high.

Our licence business model quickly involves significant amounts because we scale with production. Accordingly, the lower limit of €500,000 seemed quite appropriate to us, even if it is still a long way from the 10 % of the contract value. Although we had structured the contracts accordingly, understood every detail and agreed to the consequences in the event of a dispute, i.e. were ready to sign a joint declaration of intent, we were surprised by a decisive note from our lawyer: In the event that the negotiations fail – i.e. precisely in the case for which the »break-up fee« is intended – the reference for assessing an appropriate amount no longer applies. This is precisely when the promised, significantly higher licence agreement no longer applies. The only thing that matters is what the service received is worth. In concrete terms: what the inspection is worth to the interested party. If there were to be a legal dispute about the payment of the break-up fee, and this is not unlikely if the negotiations fail in view of the amount of the break-up fee, this amount would not be enforceable due to the lack of proportionality to the service received. The intended purpose would therefore not be fulfilled with this agreement. On the contrary: due to the lack of contractual enforceability, the signature by the interested party loses the probative value of the sincerity of the interest, because this knowledge can also be assumed on the part of the interested party. The »break-up fee« is therefore an instrument that we hear about time and again, but which is completely unsuitable for our business model.

We have therefore found a different solution: We have set up a data room in which we have stored, in a structured form. those documents that we would like to make available for due diligence by an interested party on the basis of a framework agreement. Any questions that are not answered by the data in the data room can be directed to us. However, there is a charge for answering them. This is based on the billing of consultant days for each day or part thereof. If the interested party sends a question every day, each question costs one consultant day. If a prospective customer requests extensive test material, the prospective customer can ask us for a corresponding chargeable offer. If we wish to make this offer, we will also receive appropriate compensation for this service. For us, this interpretation fulfils its purpose in several respects: we have significantly reduced our due diligence cost through standardisation, we have attached a price tag to the additional cost of queries through a consultant's daily rate for each day or part thereof, and we have put a stop to the request for further technical documents and evidence as a chargeable bar. On the negotiation side, we have thus lost the weight of a »break-up fee« and can focus on joint success on the basis of clear structures.

What it's all about

Contracts are a matter for the boss. Whether you like it or not. You are liable for your company, so you should also know what contractual obligations you have entered into for your company and what contractual rights your company is entitled to as a result. There are no excuses for this.

Every single contract deserves our full attention. This is just as important as our innovation itself. The quality of contracts is only decided in the event of a dispute – in other words, when it is actually already too late. If you haven't done your homework at the beginning, you may end up paying a high price – perhaps even far too high a price – in the event of a dispute. The fact that we were able to discover our HPB Solid-State Battery at all after a hostile takeover of our inventor's life's work is due to the fact that the lifelong research ban, to which our inventor was contractually bound, expired in the event of bankruptcy. This was the path chosen by the group that carried out the hostile takeover. The hostile takeover was unavoidable, while the recovery of scientific freedom was the result of clear rules that had been set at the beginning.

Every contract therefore harbours the risk of having to

accept obligations against you in the event of a dispute that are literally unbearable at that moment. So with every contract, take the trouble to read it in detail, understand it in detail, understand the consequences in detail and carefully check whether and under what conditions you are prepared to accept each of these details. Because that is the spirit of »pacta sunt servanda«. That's why contracts are a matter for the boss.

How to read

»PACTA SUNT SERVANDA«

› How do I deal with contracts – regardless of whether they are non-disclosure agreements, purchase, cooperation or sales contracts?

› Do contracts enjoy my full attention?

› Do I pay attention to the »big picture« of contracts?

› How do I deal with the details?

› Can I claim that I have carefully checked my rights and obligations in every contract?

› Can I say with every contract that I can live with the consequences if the contract fails?

› Have I ensured with every contract that my understanding has a reasonable chance of success even in the event of a legal dispute?

EXIT BEFORE ENTRY

What's inside

Financing an innovation is expensive. There are various instruments available on the capital market: Funding, debt capital and equity. The most expensive form of financing from the company's point of view is equity capital, because here you give up a lot of shares in the company for relatively little money, especially in the initial phase. The general perception is that the risk is often greater at the beginning rather than later on. This is why the company value increases over time and the »exchange rate« for equity becomes »worse«. Conversely, equity provides the favoured innovators with degrees of freedom because the total loss risk is shared and equity is a lever for funding and debt capital. Investors like to play this card. However, this episode looks at why not all equity is the same.

The episode

»I hate investors!« This is the favourite opening line of a friend from an innovation forge when he acquires capital. He deliberately arrives a little late for the meeting, appears slightly distracted and in a bad mood. His extremely positive experience with this opening is that if they stay seated afterwards, you can really talk to them.

Investors are a group of people in their own right. It would be wrong to lump them all together. However, their methods are very similar. The question is always about the risks of innovation and the innovators. A distinction is made between technology, production and market risks. Technology risks bundle those questions that revolve around whether the innovation works in principle at all. Production risks encompass all questions relating to the manufacturability of the innovation. However, the focus does not end with the readiness for series production, but also extends to the scalability of plant and mechanical engineering as well as the global availability of resources. Ultimately, investors want to hear a more or less infinite and, above all, unlimited growth story that does not recognise any »natural« limits. Market risks are considered because we have all learnt that the best technology does not always prevail. A favourite example of this is always the video standard »Video 2000«, which was better than the »VHS« standard, but could not prevail against it. The example itself shows the era from which those who still refer to it today originate. The best response to market risks in these circles is to sell out production for several years – and please do so well before the start of each production run. Production should therefore ideally be booked out for years to come through purchase commitments, so-called off-take agreements.

All of these questions follow an internal choreography: the aim is to make innovators aware of the enormous risks of their innovation, which can only be adequately reflected by a low company valuation. The higher the risks, the lower the company valuation. If possible, the company valuation should have been checked and certified by an auditor. As a rule, these are all people who are not really familiar with innovation and are risk-focussed by profession. This alone results from their liability for consulting errors. With all these risk factors, it is almost impossible to achieve an assessment that is appropriate from the innovators' point of view and also adequately reflects the actual potential of the innovation.

Another peculiarity of investors is that they set themselves rules according to which they invest. Regardless of the type and potential of the innovation, the company valuation is forced into the Procrustean bed of this set of rules. For all the non-Greeks among us, Wikipedia explains it as follows: »A Procrustean bed or bed of Procrustes is the colloquial term for a mould or scheme into which something is forced that doesn't actually fit there.« When in doubt, questions are asked and new risks are identified until the innovators accept the investor's evaluation logic in order to finally obtain the financial resources for the next step.

And this is where the real problem begins. Because before these investors get involved, they want to determine the conditions under which they can exit. The timeframe for this is usually relatively short, the financial resources are limited and the level of ambition for the innovator's performance to overcome the risks in the short term is correspondingly high. The exit of such an investor is therefore discussed before the investor enters. This is not only a slanted approach, but simply places the wrong emphasis. It is essentially about the benefits of the investment for the investor and no longer primarily about the benefits of the investment for the innovation. I am deliberately differentiating between the innovator and the innovation here, as the innovator is usually concerned with his innovation. He often puts his entire professional and, for the most part, private commitment into the service of innovation. This is why their innovation takes priority over everything else. This does not apply to the investor. From a wealth of investment opportunities, he »selects« those that appear most attractive to him. And so that he can take advantage of a particularly large number of opportunities, the capital commitment must not last too long and the exit must be regulated in a correspondingly lucrative manner. In particular, special rights such as »liquidation preference«, i.e. a preferred position in the event of a possible sale, or »preferred shares«, i.e. shares with special voting rights, or »drag along« and »tag along«, rules for the co-sale obligation of minority investors, should ensure the advantageousness of the investment for the investors. Such investors quickly lose the fun if you push for an equal and fair solution. Then there is something wrong with the innovator's risk assessment and that naturally makes people suspicious of the entire investment.

We have had countless conversations of this kind and we have consistently used our own compass. Having a solid compass of our own makes it possible to always mirror the discussions and offers to the needs of innovation without being completely clouded by the plethora of questions and doubts in the service of increasing risk to lower the value of the company. That's why I find the image of the compass so helpful. The captain of a ship can navigate, and stay on course using only his compass, even in the thickest fog. This does not prevent you from possibly encountering obstacles that you would have recognised earlier without the fog and could therefore have minimised the damage. However, the compass prevents you from veering off course.

It is therefore of crucial importance to scrutinise the objective of the speaker with every risk presented and every criticism. With our HPB Solid-State Battery, for example, we have consistently taken every criticism as an incentive to find a solution for this point too, to be able to provide answers that answer the questions posed at the outset. However, we did not »understand« the game for a long time: We should have realised that we simply could not answer countless questions at all, and therefore should have accepted the significantly lower valuation of the investors.

One particularly cheeky question was how it could be that we had a higher rating than a 100-year-old chocolate producer with square bars. The question was actually asked verbatim. My simple answer, namely that we don't produce chocolate, was good for a brief, cheerful irritation, but did nothing to change the investor's attitude.

If there are already fundamental differences in the assessment of opportunities and risks, then it is not unlikely that these will also exist on an interpersonal level and thus affect the collaboration. In my experience, investors with whom you have to discuss the exit before they get on board do not have sufficient liquidity anyway, or at least not enough interest to commit to innovation in the long term.

It is a fatal misconception that the main task of the innovator is to make the investor's exit particularly attractive so that his investment appears lucrative. This misconception is not only fatal for the innovator, but also for the investor.

The lack of a common or complementary perspective on the innovation is the main risk for the failure of an innovation on its way to the market. It is therefore the main task of the innovator to stay on course with a clear compass of their own and to find the right people to implement the innovation. They also exist – and even with an exclamation mark – on the investor side.

We have focussed on private investors right from the start. Private investors do not usually use a Procrustean bed for their investment decision. What counts for them is the innovation, the benefits for users and the environment and the people who realise this innovation. This is exactly what characterises you and your innovation. Let's not misunderstand each other: Such investors also have a lot of questions. However, unlike investors who discuss their exit with you before getting involved, private investors are actually interested in your answers, and that's a world of difference. Private investors usually give you the time to realise your innovation because they are looking at the implementation and not their exit. Gaining such people as supporters is a real pleasure and a significant benefit for everyone involved.

What it's all about

Attracting the right people significantly increases your innovation's chances of success. Along the way, you will find yourself confronted with investors who have a clear focus on the conditions for their own exit and want to force your company valuation into the Procrustean bed of their lowest possible valuation with a veritable flood of risk warnings. The demands of such investors are only associated with the associated risks for you and your innovation if you agree to them and the corresponding deal.

However, if you change your perspective on such discussions, they can offer you real added value: You can grow from the questions asked by investors who discuss their exit with you before getting involved, because every question holds up a mirror to where you currently stand with your innovation. This is a real benefit for you, because it helps you to improve your presentation and gives you valuable pointers as to which directions you can still look in.

With the support of the right investors, on the other hand, you have the chance of real success with your innovation. They ask their questions because they are interested in your answers, because they have a long-term interest in investing in you. You »only« have to learn to distinguish the right investors from the wrong ones. And there is only one strategy for this: stay the course, use your compass. This does not mean that you should not be open to possible course corrections when they present themselves. It does mean that you should consistently align all financing offers with the requirements of your innovation and not let the risk warnings and requirements of the wrong investors cloud your vision.

How to read

»EXIT BEFORE ENTRY«

› Do I have a clear compass for my innovation?

› Am I able to distinguish between good and bad investors?

› How do I ensure that I generate added value for my innovation from every investor meeting?

› Are there patterns that are anchored in my business model or process model for implementing my innovation that attract the wrong investors?

› Do I already know well enough who the right investors are for me?

› How do I ensure that the right investors dominate the discussions?

› Do I have the right people to answer all the questions so that I can act professionally and competently?

GREED EATS BRAINS

What's inside

»Greed eats brains« is an exponential function. The greater the greed, the disproportionately less reason has to say. Greed should not be confused with the dreams that arise when you realise the enormous potential that your own innovation offers. After all, this potential is one of the drivers for realisation. Greed is the ugly side of the inner drive. The side where – like Gollum in Tolkien's »Lord of the Rings« – you are prepared to do anything to gain an advantage. To take any risk, to see everyone as a potential opponent and eliminate them, and to spout more and more nonsense. Greed switches off reason, and even worse: greed kills fundamental values. This episode is about the many facets of greed and how important it is to recognise its ugly face early enough.

The episode

Innovation stirs up fears and raises hopes. Those who feel threatened by innovation and their status work purposefully against innovation. They use all the means they can muster. Due to this fear, there are no restrictions on the range of methods, no »red lines« that should not be crossed. After all, the end justifies the means. Innovation creates prosperity – and prosperity needs to be defended. Those who manage prosperity instead of creating it are dependent on securing their sinecures and keeping their source of prosperity flowing for as long as possible. Innovation is a sensitive opponent here, as this could lead to these »water rights« being redistributed and one's own source of prosperity drying up over time. This view affects not only individual companies and their leaders, but also nations. Europe, and Germany in particular, are stuck in this dilemma. Once a pioneer of innovation and the cradle of the economic miracle, the preservationists are currently winning every debate about the future.

On the other hand, there are the hopes associated with innovation. Initially, the circle of hopefuls is still manageable and is fuelled by a deep rootedness in innovation. The further the implementation progresses towards market development, the larger and more heterogeneous this circle becomes. More and more people realise the potential of this innovation – and want a slice of the pie.

For me, discovering an innovation is comparable to discovering a vein of gold on a vast plot of land. You know that you have stumbled upon enormous potential that you can never even begin to realise on your own. You need helpers and supporters who can provide you with the right tools, help you overcome obstacles and with whom you can then celebrate your joint success and enjoy the fruits of your labour. »Competition stimulates business» is one of those sayings when there is competition for positions. We all know this from the dance on the career ladder: the higher you climb, the less room there is on the rungs. The fight for the next step gets tougher and tougher. The methods used to assert yourself against the competition often become increasingly antisocial. What remains is bitterness and loneliness and a vague feeling of power. Your own frustration often invites you to take this power out on those around you: Employees, customers, family. Everyone suffers. Competition only stimulates business from the spectator's point of view. They have a box seat and can enjoy the methods used by competitors to try and outdo each other. Competition is the antithesis of co-operation. Before you help an »opponent«, you prefer to accept a »loss« yourself, which you assume will hit you less hard than refusing to help your »opponent«, and before you know it, you're fighting alone on a wide front. The downward spiral begins.

The discovery of our HPB Solid-State Electrolyte and thus our HPB Solid-State Battery is one such goldmine. We know that we are dependent on helpers for the success of our technology. We see the sheer immeasurable potential in the broad range of applications as well as the energy and mobility transition. That is why we have designed our business model with common sense. Instead of indulging in the omnipotence fantasy that we can do everything on our own if we only think big enough, we have opted for a licence business model. In the image of the vein of gold on a vast plot of land, we sit in a down-to-earth forest pub and offer our partners four stakes to stake their claim. In this way, they can help to unearth this vein of gold. The special thing about our claims is that we only make them big enough for our licence holders to exploit the potential. And we distribute each claim without any overlaps. This means that we licence our technology according to fields of application and geographies for stationary applications, for example for "home storage in Germany". We also grant production licences because not everyone who can develop a field of application also wants to become a battery manufacturer. Finally, we grant licences to the automotive industry to use our HPB Solid-State Electrolyte for their battery development. By sharing our gold vein in this way, our licensees benefit from a licence that gives them the opportunity to leverage the potential of our HPB Technology in their area of expertise. We retain our role as a technology developer and do not compete with our licensees. The division of our claims favours cooperation between us, because competition only exists externally. And even externally, we communicate the benefits of a global energy and mobility transition for the development of our societies and the protection of the environment, because we are convinced that our technology can stake a claim to an overarching golden vein that is centred around the creation of better living and environmental conditions. Here, too, the principle applies that co-operation can achieve more than isolation and greed.

Could we solve greed at its root through this structure of our actions? Certainly not. Greed is too complex for that. However, we now know how to recognise the ugly face of greed at a very early stage. The first sign of greed is detachment. This involves glorifying one's own achievements and abilities on the one hand, and more or less systematically belittling the abilities of potential »competitors« on the other. Another characteristic of greed is speed. If everything suddenly has to happen very quickly because the joint opportunity is so great, the opportunity is so unique and the network of supporters is as shy as a deer, extreme caution is required. This is when established relationships should be abandoned, principles thrown overboard and, ideally, everything put on one card. Trust is replaced by »experience«. There is only one risk on the way to realising this particular opportunity, namely the risk of the innovator faltering.

In such situations, you suddenly feel lonely and abandoned. You ask yourself whether there are two white lights coming towards you on the motorway or hundreds. Who is the ghost driver here? Then it helps to think back to the core of your own innovation, your own path, your original potential and, above all, your own values. It helps to evaluate the opportunity in the same way as an opportunity that seems much smaller. Why should you work less carefully with a huge opportunity than with a small one? Which networks and collaborations have ensured stability in the realisation to date? Which partners were important and should remain so?

The exponential function of »greed eats brains« becomes particularly clear when people boast about who they know. Everything happens extremely quickly until the commission negotiation is finalised. The phone is constantly ringing, new emails are constantly arriving and your own reaction speed is nowhere near enough to keep up with the new speed of realisation. And then? Silence. Suddenly it becomes clear that you have to do your homework to realise the biggest opportunity. It is not enough to blow up the opportunity. You also have to deliver. How often have we been asked to remove »disruptive« people from our network? They would unjustifiably lay a hand on our vein of gold, even though their contribution was obviously so small. But it is regularly partnerships that carry us, that have gone through thick and thin with us. You don't leave such companions behind. Such companions deserve our trust and our invitation to celebrate our joint success. Those who underestimate this, who belittle it, wear the ugly grimace of greed proudly in front of their face and yet only see the shining all-rounder in the mirror. This grimace becomes even uglier when the keyboard of slander is played in addition to the disparagement.

When the network and the relationships seem all too glorious and the potential is systematically placed far beyond one's imagination, then it is time for care and caution. Then it is time to step out of loneliness and isolation and, with your true confidants, with your companions, re-establish your stability, stand by your values and convictions and extend the invitation to cook together on a meaningful flame. Greed can be cured at an early stage. It can therefore be worthwhile to reach out with clarity for honest, genuine cooperation.

What it's all about

You will have countless conversations along the way. Many of these conversations will centre around funding and the potential of your innovation. Realise that greed tempts you to go in the wrong direction, to stray from the path, to take risks that you would never be willing to take without greed. Then it is time to pause for thought. Time to check your own foundations. Time to evaluate the offered direction of co-operation, completely detached from the possible outcome. Is that what you want? Do you want it this way? Are you prepared to pay the price? These are questions that you should not answer alone. Ask the questions of your companions. Seek advice from people you trust deeply. Because time pressure and glorious prospects are a dangerous cocktail, sweet and numbing and with a heavy hangover after the high.

You recognise greed when every anchor of reason is lifted before it hits solid ground. When your speed is supposedly far too slow. And when you should just let the others do it, because they've already done it umpteen times. Then you should remain vigilant. Carry out your check just as carefully as you would if you had a smaller chance. Then you should put yourself in a state of alert that you would feel in the event of an obvious attack. Because greed is a danger to your innovation, a danger to you. Greed is never associated with a real opportunity. Greed destroys and divides everyt-hing that is and should remain important to you. Even and especially with growing success.

How to read

»GREED EATS BRAINS«

› Who are my companions that I trust 100 %?

› How susceptible am I myself to greed?

› Do I regularly check myself to see whether I am affected by greed and thus jeopardising my innovation?

› Are there people around me who I can recognise as harbingers of greed?

› Am I making the occurrence of greed sufficiently transparent?

› Am I sufficiently involving the victims of greed, my companions, in the defence against greed?

› What is my offer to nip greed in the bud and offer genuine co-operation if the person concerned appears »curable«?

THE ENEMY IN MY BED

What's inside

People like to let their gaze wander. Especially when it comes to finding reasons for the failure of an innovation. Reasons for their own failure. The culprits are quickly identified: it's the environmental conditions, the framework conditions, other players in the market environment, and so on and so forth. In short: it's the others. But what if the problems are much closer to home? What if they are rooted in your own team? Then failure is no longer a fate, but a creeping process that should be countered as early as possible. This episode looks at why this realisation is obvious, but why solving the problem is sometimes so difficult.

The episode

Every person is different. Even twins are not the same. Everyone has their own individual strengths and weaknesses, things that drive them, things that slow them down. Every person has specific conditions under which they feel particularly comfortable, under which they are at their best. This applies not only to their professional field of activity, but also to their private life. Days on which people feel good feel easy, offer more joy than stress and make people shine overall. On the other hand, days on which a person does not feel good, feel heavy, worries and hardships dominate and the person is more irritable than relaxed. This is human and a good thing. Because it offers the opportunity to scrutinise yourself and get to the bottom of the possible causes of your bad mood.

If you look at the context of teams from an individual perspective, it is easy to see that it can happen every day in any team that people who are feeling good meet people who are not feeling good. These are the days when arguments occur, days when things can get heated. Every argument harbours the risk of injuries that can leave scars. Scars on the team's soul. Preventing every dispute is an unattainable ideal. However, it is negligent to accept arguments as »normal« and thereby deprive yourself of the opportunity to discover potential problems. It is completely irrelevant in which hierarchical constellation and direction these disputes occur. Often, minor quarrels resolve themselves. It becomes problematic when a creeping alienation takes place. At some point, this alienation also affects innovation – and in the worst-case scenario, it hits them with full force.

When people turn away from each other to such an extent

that further collaboration seems impossible, when sensitivities outweigh the benefits of collaboration, then unfortunately it is often too late. This is when competences that are helpful for the implementation of the innovation are lost. It seems obvious to appease before this point. To call on everyone involved to be level-headed, to swear them to the common goal. But that is not enough. There are chasms in each and every one of us that we cannot overcome ourselves. So how can an outsider ask us to ignore or even overcome these abysses?

This is the moment when leadership matters. Leadership is not to be understood in a simplified sense as the beat on the galley. Leadership is a multi-layered art. Natural leadership is when people are willing to follow – even when the going gets tough. That is why leadership is inextricably linked to responsibility. Responsibility that goes far beyond the function. Responsibility that you actively take on.

Whether geopolitics or team conflict, the pattern is always the same. Starting a conflict is relatively easy. Ending a conflict, on the other hand, all too often seems impossible. It starts with an unspoken conflict. A negative experience, a dissatisfaction, a doubt. The cause of such conflicts is not always where they come to light as an open conflict. Then you see superficial lines of conflict that are actually proxy conflicts. »Young versus old« is one such proxy conflict. Especially when the implementation of an innovation takes much longer than expected. It is then difficult for the »first generation« to accept that things have not worked out as planned. So why should a »second generation« be lucky enough to be able to master the challenge? Instead of complementing each other's skills and experience, we end up in a pseudo-conflict of »young versus old«. Prejudices and sensitivities also all too often dominate the willingness of the existing team to take on new employees. Examples of these internal sources of conflict are a dime a dozen.

Clarity and consistency through leadership and acceptance of responsibility are relevant for resolving these lines of conflict. Just as every person is unique, every person is also replaceable. This clarity is necessary to avoid becoming hostage to internal sensitivities. Nobody should be able to allow innovation to fail because of their own sensitivities. It is then necessary to clarify the competences that could be lost in the »worst case scenario« of separation for the successful implementation of the innovation. There are people out there who do not share these conflict lines and can bring the necessary competences with them. This responsibility also necessarily includes their own role. If I myself become a brake on implementation, I should vacate my position in the interests of innovation so that someone else can fulfil this task better. Those who point the finger at others often fail to realise that they are pointing three fingers at themselves.

In terms of leadership skills, this means looking behind the lines of conflict with an alert eye, taking the time to understand the actual causes, helping to resolve them and, in case of doubt, being prepared to draw the necessary consequences for innovation. Without consistency, leadership is nothing – with consistency, leadership is a rock in the face of challenges. Innovation has the »disadvantage« that nobody has done it before. That's why the challenges are individual and unpredictable. I see the diversity of people as a gift and an enrichment. However, I am also very clear about drawing the line when individual conflicts threaten the realisation of innovation.

In the event that it becomes necessary to draw the consequences of a separation, there is another component that I believe is essential for success. It is the way in which you separate. Because true greatness is revealed in the separation. It's not about drawing a line as radically as possible at the end of a shared journey. It's not about one being right and the other wrong, one being good and the other guilty. It is about recognising and appreciating what we have achieved together for the further development of innovation. This does not prevent dirty laundry from being washed. But it does offer the opportunity to treat each other with dignity and wish each other all the best for the future. Anyone who misunderstands this as a »method« or »instrument« of leadership will be exposed. Because the gestures in the separation are only effective if they are authentic. Only then do they unfold their own power, which, despite the separation, fills in the gaps that previously seemed insurmountable.

What it's all about

A good working atmosphere is the backbone of a successful company. Then everyone plays in top form in every position and according to their individual capabilities. Then everyone gives their best for the common success. However, the working atmosphere is exposed to numerous attacks every day due to all our individuality and numerous external influences. Leadership then acts like an immune system: an open ear, an embracing gesture, a nudge in the right direction is often enough.

However, if this is not enough, then leadership must

encapsulate the problem through clarity and, in case of doubt, protect the innovation through a separation. This is the moment when human leadership takes on a special significance: the separation is not just a personal matter between the company and the person concerned. The manner in which the separation is handled also has an impact on the working atmosphere. This aspect and its effect can only be underestimated. It is worthwhile to constantly observe the working atmosphere with sensitivity and empathy, to recognise distortions and lines of conflict in good time and, in case of doubt, to resolve them clearly and consistently. After all, the relevant benchmark is the success of your innovation – without causing internal devastation.

How to read

»THE ENEMY IN MY BED«

› Do I have a clear enough view of the inner lines of conflict in my innovation?

› Do I have a good enough feeling about the causes of these lines of conflict?

› How do I deal with conflicts?

› Is a good working atmosphere my boss's business?

› What do I offer to resolve conflicts at an early stage?

› Am I prepared to draw the consequences?

› Am I sufficiently aware of the positive ripple effects of clarity and consistency in conjunction with human leadership?

THE POWER OF THE BURN RATE

What's inside

The »burn rate« describes the monthly capital requirement of a company. It is the answer to the question of how much money a company is »burning« as long as it is not yet in the profit zone. It is therefore a very simple key figure that investors regularly ask about. In this episode, we look at what this question is actually about, which question follows it and how problematic the investor's final decision based on it can be.

The episode

Innovations usually cost money before they earn money. In this phase, the company »burns« investment funds for people, machines and materials. The more established the innovation activity is, the more continuous and therefore predictable this »burn rate« is. It often increases over time before the first sales lead to profits.

For investors, information about capital requirements is of crucial importance. After all, the »burn rate« says a lot about the company's future capital requirements. However, it says nothing about the quality of the utilisation of funds, about whether the company's goals are being achieved efficiently or effectively. Goals are achieved efficiently if the investments are as proportionate as possible to the progress made. Goals are achieved effectively when »all guns are blazing«, when people, machines and materials are put on the ramp in almost any quantity in order to achieve the set goal.

In dialogue with investors, the plot around the burn rate usually follows the following pattern: What is your current burn rate and what milestones do you plan to achieve by when? What advantages would be conceivable from your perspective if you were to overcome the financial restriction with fresh investment capital? This combination imperceptibly raises the bar. More money, more milestones in less time. That's the simple formula. However, this quickly becomes a fine line. After all, building up a team's new capabilities, be it through more people, more machines or more material, is associated with specific challenges that often take time. And it is precisely this time that needs to be shortened. Stress and running costs increase, errors creep in. The advantage of better capitalisation in the short term becomes a burden that can fall on the innovator's shoulders. Because the next time capital is raised, the same questions arise. The hamster wheel spins faster and faster.

Another plot centred around the »burn rate« is particularly popular with »would-be« investors. These are the »bargain hunters«, the »smart ones« among investors. Because they are not really interested in the milestones that can be reached with the current »burn rate«. They are interested in how long the money will last before it is burnt. That's why they ask about the current account balance. The three-sentence answer »account balance divided by the burn rate equals negotiation time« is the start of a sheer abundance of sham discussions in which the investment interest is kept high throughout, but the sand runs through the clock to inevitably reach the point of the innovator's greatest need, the impending collapse of the company. Then the time has come when the original valuation at which the investor could have imagined buying in no longer seems tenable, indeed far too high. The »exchange rate« rises – entirely in the investor's favour.

This path can be recognised by the fact that such investors ask quite directly about the »burn rate«. Long before they have had a chance to substantially analyse the innovation, the business model and its possible contributions to success. Because we know the choreography of such discussions, we consistently choose a radical shortcut: when asked about our burn rate, we say that we are efficiently achieving our milestones. We do not state the actual amount. We also state this clearly and give reasons for it. This is because we refer to the immediate next question about the account balance and the foreseeable triple rate for the duration of the negotiations. That makes sense. Sometimes it doesn't feel good for the potential investor either. This open manner gives pause for thought and encourages reflection. In any case, this is where the wheat is separated from the chaff. The genuinely interested investors jump to the innovation side, while the »bargain hunters« point out how negligent it is to react in this way. This is also efficient – namely in dealing with your own resources.

What it's all about

The burn rate is about nothing less than the survival of innovation. However, it is also an instrument in the hands of investors. On the one hand, many investors expect their investment to increase the speed at which they reach their goal. This often results in a higher demand for people, machines and materials. On the other hand, the »burn rate« in conjunction with the account balance is a valuable indication of how long the negotiation has to be »stretched out« in order to achieve a more favourable entry price. This is primarily about the company's liquidity and therefore the chances of realisation and survival of the innovation. In reality, however, it is always about winning over the right people to support the innovation. And the right people are first and foremost interested in the innovation and the innovators.

For you and your innovation, this means that you should pay full attention to every investor meeting. Pay attention to the mould from which the person in front of you is cast. Go beyond the superficial level and take a look behind the scenes. Fathom the investor's real interest. Innovators are often so enthusiastic about their idea that they do not sufficiently analyse what the investors' actual interests are. The more attentively you analyse the motives of the investors, the quicker you can identify the right people. If it's all about the numbers, you're the next money-printing machine – provided you deliver sensibly on the hamster wheel. Such conversations tend to have a justifying character. They lack impulse. You feel grilled. Unmistakable signs of a difficult relationship after the investment. The clearer you are about your goals and the path to achieving them, the greater your charisma. This is what should convince investors of you and your innovation.

How to read

»THE POWER OF THE BURN RATE«

› Do I know my »burn rate« in detail?

› Is my »burn rate« efficient or effective?

› How quickly does the interested investor ask about the »burn rate«?

› Am I already on the hamster wheel?

› How do I feel when I imagine no longer discussing the »burn rate« at the first appointment?

› Am I sufficiently clear about how the upcoming investment and its conditions will affect my »burn rate«?

› Am I sufficiently aware of the consequences of a higher level of ambition?

SEX/RISK/BRAND

What's inside

There are innovations and innovators who seem to manage their own financing effortlessly. Other innovations and innovators, on the other hand, find it difficult. This seems all the more incomprehensible the closer the innovations are to each other, for example if they come from the same technology environment. If you analyse in detail what exactly the differences between the innovations are, three decisive factors crystallise: sex, risk and brand. This episode looks at what this is all about.

The episode

Investors often decide which opportunity they want to back from a veritable plethora of investment projects. In doing so, they are often supported by advisors who make an investment recommendation or directly on behalf of the investors and within the framework of their decision parameters. Every decision carries the risk of a possible total loss. If you don't invest your own money, you have to justify why you backed the wrong horse. Couldn't or shouldn't you have recognised this? How would others have decided? It's about pulling your head out of the noose. Losses hurt and must be avoided as much as possible. If they do occur, it's better not to be one of the guilty parties.

But what are the criteria that provide the best possible justification for the investment decision? These criteria should be as unassailable as possible. Criteria that anyone else would confirm that they would also have decided in favour of the investment on the basis of them.

We were able to compare this in the area of solid-state battery projects and came across three criteria that can plausibly explain the differences in the appeal of one innovation compared to another. We were sent a presentation, a pitch deck, so that we could see what we could improve in our storytelling. Technologically, the main difference was the solid-state electrolyte, the electrolyte of a solid-state battery, a fundamentally different chemistry. The level of investment they were aiming for matched ours. Our level of maturity was already much more advanced. The performance and manufacturability independently documented by the Fraunhofer Institute were also better for us than for the other technology. The higher appeal of the other innovation could therefore not be attributed to the technology itself. That would have been reason enough to »dismiss« the pitch deck and simply put it aside. Nevertheless, we challenged ourselves to understand the real drivers.

We noticed three major differences in the results, which we summarised somewhat luridly as the criteria »sex«, »risk« and »brand«. The first striking difference related to the management team: highly qualified women were pitted against middle-aged white men. An »eye-catcher« in a male-dominated technology environment, and that is by no means meant in a sexist way. Another characteristic difference was the technological risk: if the basic functional principle had to be proven with the investment in one project, it was a matter of producing the first production line at our company. This difference naturally had a serious impact on the company valuation, which was much lower for the one project than for us. So there was more »share« for the same capital. This difference in the company valuation is even understandable. The further the route, the higher the realisation risks and the lower the company value. The third key difference was the utilisation of a strong brand behind the spin-off of one project. We do not have access to such a strong brand. To summarise, the sex-risk-brand formula emerged as the driver of the appeal of one innovation over another. We do not have these three factors.

Back to the justification for the investment decision. Ideally, the selection process is about choosing the projects with the highest returns and the best hit rate. The decisive factor here is not how far the innovation has progressed. It is not about the certainty of realisability and scalability. Rather, it is about the leverage for your own investment and the »neutral« reasons why any other portfolio manager would have decided in favour of the project. Every investment in an innovation harbours the risk of total loss. It is almost impossible to predict which innovation will succeed and which will fail.

In our comparison, the identical total loss risk – because the same investment sums were involved – was therefore offset by different potential returns. These are a question of the share in the company. The calculation is comparatively simple: a larger slice of the cake means a larger share of the profits. This is a generalised assessment. It is as correct as it is wrong, because it is impossible to predict the exact success anyway. As a result, all that remains is to compare the pieces of the pie, i.e. the shares in the company that are acquired with the investment.

An example from the casino illustrates the effect and thus the obvious portfolio decision. To do this, we compare two opposing strategies in roulette: The bet on »red« or »black« against the same bet on the »34«, for example. Both strategies carry the risk of total loss. The »red/black« strategy has a probability of occurrence of almost 50 %, as only the zero is green and the remaining 36 numbers are equally black or red. The »34«, on the other hand, only has a probability of 1:37. The total loss risk of the »red/black« strategy is therefore considerably lower. On the other hand, a hit with the »red/black« strategy doubles the stake, whereas a hit with the »34« is rewarded with a factor of 36. So while the risk of total loss is identical for both strategies, the thrill of success with the »34« strategy is incomparable.

Early-stage investors are looking for that kick, that high leverage. In return, they are prepared to take considerable risks. The more clearly the innovators stand out from other innovators – in our example, highly qualified women instead of middle-aged white men – and the stronger the brand behind it is, the higher the probability of success is estimated to be, because it lends a reputation and makes failure less likely from a neutral perspective. In this risk assessment, a project where the homework has been done and the technical risk is therefore low, but which also lacks an outstanding management team and a strong, well-known brand, is simply less attractive than one that scores better in these categories. »Sex«, »risk« and »brand« are therefore relevant categories that should be taken seriously when competing for the financial resources to realise your own innovation.

What it's all about

In the competition for investments in innovation, it's all about the appeal of innovation. It serves to justify the investor's portfolio decision and should be assessable and comprehensible using neutral criteria. »Sex«, »risk« and »brand« are perhaps the most important criteria over which the innovator often has only limited influencc. However, it is a decisive advantage to know these criteria and take them seriously.

This involves relevant fundamental decisions. It is about deciding whether, and on what terms you want to involve a partner with a strong brand in order to fulfil the »brand« criterion. It is also about the fundamental decision as to when you want to collect how much investment capital from which partners and under what conditions. You must be aware that the lower your risk, i.e. the better you have done your »homework«, the fewer partners you will find from the venture capital sector. There is therefore a dependency, a trade-off, between the capital acquisition costs – i.e. how many shares you have to give up – and the acquisition offers – i.e. how many investors make you an offer at all. You therefore need to take care of your investor strategy in good time. The »sex« category is best described as external impact. It is not exclusively dependent on gender. It is also a question of presentation. How »attractive« is your packaging? Here, too, it is worth investing in professional support in good time, either by commissioning it or hiring it.

Without »sex«, »risk« and »brand«, innovation is simply boring for many investors. But pay attention to your DNA, because that is ultimately responsible for your authenticity. That is a radiance that you cannot buy, and your DNA should never be for sale. This radiance lies within you. And at the end of the day, it is no less important than the bold categories of »sex«, »risk« and »brand«.

How to read

»SEX/RISK/BRAND«

› What appeal does my innovation have?

› What appeal does my founding team have?

› Do I have a strong brand in the background or on what terms am I prepared to close this gap?

› What risk do I have and when, and how does this fit in with my investor strategy?

› Have I already invested enough in the attractiveness of my innovation's public image?

› Do I know my DNA and do my ideas for closing gaps in the »sex«, »risk« and »brand« categories match it?

› Can I justify the reasons for my choices in the categories »sex«, »risk« and »brand« in a comprehensible way?

THREE TIMES NO

What's inside

Investors set themselves investment rules. These rules correspond to the translation of their own investment strategy. As a rule, however, they are not made transparent to the innovator. In principle, the investor can imagine many things and can afford almost anything. They also have an enormous network, and the skills needed to make the innovation a success. This episode looks at why it is good to review these rules as early as possible.

The episode

The TV format »Die Höhle der Löwen« (e.g. »Shark Tank«) enjoys a certain popularity not only in Germany. On the one hand, you are presented with many exciting new ideas, while on the other you can watch the strategies the innovators use to convince the »lions«. For me, this programme regularly creates a disturbing feeling. At the latest when it comes to the deal offers following the presentation, it becomes clear what an enormous gap there is between the »lions« and the innovators. It is rarely about larger investments, i.e. investments above the million mark, and even more rarely about larger valuations. This may be due to the pre-selection of innovations that are approved for this format. However, it is noticeable that it is regularly about relatively large shares in the companies that the »lions« want to invest in.

The personal commitment of the investor is added to the investment sum as a »monetary benefit«, which is why the size of the company share and the low company valuation are even sold as »accommodating«. In view of the fame and attractive self-confidence of the »lions«, this commitment seems enormous, but to be honest, it cannot be quantified at all. After all, not every deal is a success.

Another disturbing television format is »Das Supertalent« (e.g. »America's Got Talent«) or, interchangeably, »Deutschland sucht den Superstar« (e.g. »American Idol«). Here, a jury of celebrities judges candidates, some of whom expose themselves to the point of complete self-abandonment. As if that wasn't bad enough, the more lurid and hurtful the feedback is, the louder the audience roars. »Three times no« is the receipt for the now socially stigmatised »losers«.

The combination of these two formats on the innovator's side is exciting. It sounds cheeky, and it is. If you are aware of the choreography and the objectives behind it, requests of this kind are about building up an enormous gap, which in the best-case scenario results in a favour, namely a very favourable deal for investors who are willing to stake their reputation for innovation.

That's exactly what happened to us. We were called by one of the »lions« because they were interested in investing in our battery innovation. Of course, you feel honoured when such investors approach you on their own initiative. After all, we hadn't even tried or applied for it. With the knowledge of the format and the associated feeling of disruption, we asked about the conditions for the investment before any further exchange of content and after expressing our sincere thanks for the interest. We were assured that this was unusual. It is customary for the conditions to only emerge at the end of the due diligence process, i.e. after the innovation has been evaluated in detail. However, this explanation seemed too one-sided to us. After all, a detailed due diligence is also associated with an enormous amount of work for us. And it is always new. Every investor has their very own way of checking and scrutinising the »*status quo*«. Accordingly, no two due diligences are the same.

That is why we have adopted the efficient position for both sides that, on the one hand, the terms of the offer are already determined in advance because the investor has a clear internal investment strategy, and these terms of the offer are »translated« from the due diligence to the individual case. The result is always the same, it just feels customised for the innovator because the rationale is tailored to their innovation. On the other hand, our point of view, which was efficient for both sides, concerned the clarity that the effort of an extensive due diligence is only worthwhile for both sides if the terms of the offer are within a fundamental area of agreement. This argument was apparently so convincing that the »lion« decided to actually specify these conditions to us in advance: »We get 20 % of the company. In return, we will give up to €1.5 million. And we'll provide the operational management.« Our answer came immediately: »Three times no.«

At that time, we had already sold our shares to private investors at a company valuation of €53 million. The valuation of »20 %« with an investment of »up to €1.5 million« results in a valuation of €7.5 million in the most favourable case from an innovator's point of view. And that with an investment sum that is too much to die for and too little to live for. If you then take into account that the operational management is essentially a controlling body in the sense of the investor and not necessarily the »perfect fit« for the successful implementation of the innovation, then these three conditions are far away from any agreement corridor.

The exciting experience of this conversation concerned two aspects for which we are deeply grateful and which made a deep impression on us: In the short term, it was completely understandable for both sides that the effort of due diligence would not be worthwhile with these opposing positions. And we therefore sincerely and amicably wished each other every success for our respective projects. In the medium term, we had two further rounds with the same »lion«, each of which was preceded by an increase in the value of the company on our part. A brief comparison of the investment criteria revealed that the investment criteria had not changed. The friendly position of going our separate ways remained unchanged. We liked this so much that we actively networked other innovators who still fitted into the corridor of these criteria with this »lion«. In our view, that is appreciation at eye level.

What it's all about

Due diligence involves a great deal of effort for everyone involved. This makes it all the more sensible to clarify in advance which basic investment conditions are to be expected in the investor's offer corridor. This involves the specific investment amount on the one hand and the targeted »exchange rate«, i.e. the company valuation, on the other. Believe me, in most cases these conditions are already fixed before your exchange. So don't hesitate to ask about these conditions in advance. If you don't receive an answer, you should share your view of your company valuation and make your investment conditions transparent. Then you can avoid a nonsensical effort.

Without transparency about the investor's investment conditions, it is not always possible to avoid this expense. However, transparency about your conditions helps you to maintain your composure when explaining your rejection. We have also experienced this: When, at the end of a really exhausting due diligence process, the offer was far below our originally communicated deal structure and even significantly below the valuation that resulted from the joint work on the business case including VAT effect modulation (i.e adjusting for VAT impact), we cancelled the deal without further ado. The investor's financial advisor was outraged and extremely annoyed. We sincerely reciprocated this feeling. After all, we agreed on the valuation and then had a sharp disagreement on the offer. When the investor called me, irritated, he opened the conversation by asking if we were still in love. I could honestly answer in the affirmative. I was able to answer his question as to how we would get together by referring to our existing offer, which was still realisation-oriented. But when he then tried to explain again that he had explained in detail why we would only get together on the basis of his offer, I heard myself say: »Then I'm afraid we'll have to have a long-distance relationship.«

This straightforwardness may seem brusque, but it also prevents the wrong investors from coming on board. If a solution seems bad, it doesn't get better because there may not be an alternative in the short term. »Where one door closes, another opens«, as the old saying goes. I would add: If you go through the wrong door, you might not come back.

How to read

»THREE TIMES NO«

› Do I have the confidence to enter into negotiations with investors on an equal footing?

› Are the conditions clear to me in good time?

› Can I check whether the services offered actually provide added value for my innovation?

› Do the investor's investment criteria match my objectives?

› Do I know which documents I can and would like to submit for review and inspection of the »*status quo*« as part of a due diligence?

› Do I have the feeling that a gap is being created between the investor and me?

› Am I sufficiently transparent and clear in my ideas?

CORONA AND MONEY

What's inside

The coronavirus pandemic has shown us how quickly threatening diseases can spread. It has also shown us that nature has been merciful to us so far. The virus has become less aggressive over time and is now just an annoying cold that we will all catch from time to time, but from which only a few will die. Like any viral disease, coronavirus also has one essential element without which its spread would be unthinkable: the next host. If the next host did not exist, sooner or later the immune system of the infected person would gain the upper hand and render the virus harmless, or the virus would gain the upper hand over the host. This episode is about what corona has to do with money.

The episode

According to the definition in the Gabler Business Dictionary, money is »the generally recognised means of exchange and payment that a society has agreed upon. If one is obliged by the legal system to accept the money, it serves as legal tender through which a debt can be repaid with legal effect.« The creation of money is the task of the state, on whose behalf «cash« is produced. Coins minted in metal or banknotes printed on paper together form the means of payment. Because the creation of money is a sovereign task of the state, it is prohibited to produce money yourself. Nevertheless, the idea of becoming fabulously rich is extremely appealing to many people.

But how can I do that if I can't print my own money? Then I have to try to increase my economic assets through skilful barter transactions so that I become richer and richer. The acquisition of company shares offers particular leverage. They have the chance to multiply their value in a short space of time. You just have to back the right idea and then a small investment can turn into a large fortune. The early investors in Amazon are now multi-millionaires – if they have stuck with it.

And this is exactly where the patterns of corona and money meet. The spread of a virus, i.e. its multiplication, necessarily requires transmission from one host to the next. Transferred to the multiplication of money, the most likely, and by that we mean the most promising, version is an investment in a successful innovation. So, if we rule out the lottery or a rich inheritance as a strategy for spontaneous money multiplication, money needs a special host to multiply. And this host is the idea. The special thing about this realisation is that coronavirus and money share the same pattern: Viral pressure is quite high everywhere in our environment. Our immune system has developed defence strategies that get many viruses under control before we even realise that we have been attacked. This means that not every virus has the evolutionary luck to be able to multiply successfully once it has landed in its new host. If you believe the analysts, the money for innovation is on the street. However, every innovator can tell you a thing or two about how difficult it is to bring investors and innovators together. The good realisation remains that money is the virus and the host is the innovation.

What it's all about

The healthier your immune system is, the easier it is for you to defend yourself against harmful external influences. If you realise this biological fact and apply it to the money system, you will find that money behaves like a virus: Money needs a host for its own reproduction. The most attractive host is and remains a good idea, an innovation. It offers the investor the chance to increase his money considerably in a very short time with a manageable risk.

Not all money is the same – just as not all viruses are the same. Your immune system is in your DNA – this applies to your body as well as to your innovation and your company. Viruses that attack your DNA are particularly dangerous. It is therefore important to recognise in good time which money is good and which is harmful. This can only be done by analysing investors and investment conditions in a relentlessly transparent manner.

If the money for innovation is actually on the street, then the bottleneck factor is innovation. Then your innovation is the asset, not the money. But even if the money for your innovation is not on the street, it is no less damaging to your innovation if it attacks your DNA.

How to read

»CORONA AND MONEY«

› Am I sufficiently aware that my innovation is the asset and not the money?

› How do I make sure that I use this knowledge to create a level playing field between innovation and investment?

› How robust is my innovation DNA?

› How robust is my corporate DNA?

› How do I ensure that the rules of investment do not undermine the DNA of my innovation?

› How can I prevent this awareness from making me feel superior?

› How can I use the analogy between coronavirus and money to boost the appeal of my innovation?

INTERMEDIARIES AND FREE RIDERS

What's inside

Innovation creates fascination. It creates a veritable gold-rush atmosphere. As soon as an innovation achieves a significant breakthrough, or is suspected of being able to achieve one, a huge number of people suddenly appear out of nowhere and want to contribute to its success. They know an incredible number of people who have an incredible amount of wealth and are prepared to make their contribution, ideally in return for a success fee. If you listen to them, the money is on the street and success is just a stone's throw away. All too often, disillusionment comes very quickly. The contacts are not resilient, and suddenly everything is more complicated than expected. This episode looks at what you should look out for when selecting intermediaries and how you can separate the wheat from the chaff at an early stage.

The episode

We all know them: people who seem to know God and the world. They throw around familiar names and matching stories. All wealthy people are personally known, their children have attended the same school as their own children, they are closely connected to the family and can only be inspired for innovation through these people. »Name dropping« is the name of this sport, and it is difficult fare for the listener as they get to know each other.

In a nutshell, it is only a matter of hours before all financing issues for the innovation are resolved. That is why it is important to define the conditions in advance. All too often, innovators disappoint when, having achieved success, they forget the crucial contributions made by intermediaries and can no longer remember any remuneration agreements.

So a round of negotiating conditions begins. This is often accompanied by discussions about »retainers«, which are monthly payments on account of success, travelling expenses, which are of course not covered by the commission, and exclusivities – after all, you want to avoid double acquisitions. As a rule, a list of targets is not provided, as this means that you are handing over your asset as an agent: The contact list. Mutual trust has to grow first. The more »early-stage« the company, the higher the commission demands are, of course, as the blind effort for the agents is naturally higher and much more difficult to calculate due to risk-averse contacts. Such negotiations sometimes even extend over several contract versions. After all, based on his negative experiences with other innovators, the intermediary must be sure that all conditions are securely agreed under all circumstances.

Once this phase is over, the next phase in the brokerage process begins: the broker's learning curve. With a high level of commitment, all conceivable questions from the »critical investor« are anticipated and all documents are scrutinised. They constantly scrutinise why no one else has come up with this innovation before. No information is sufficient, everything can of course be done better. Simply put, it consumes an incredible amount of time for the innovator. Incidentally, in this context I regularly find it admirable how much intermediaries in particular can memorise – and without making any notes of their own. It can make you enviously doubt your own abilities.

In the next phase of »swarming«, the point of disillusionment comes relatively quickly. The contacts are initially very interested, but then ask the expected critical questions and are not satisfied with the answers. The acquisition success fails to materialise. Frustration grows. The agent's impetus grows accordingly, namely to the effect that there are significant weaknesses in the current set-up on the part of the innovators. If these are not rectified immediately in line with the feedback from critical investors, the marketability of the innovation erodes. An appeal is made to the innovator's insight.

If you look at this process from a certain distance, you realise two things: firstly, this pattern is the rule and not the exception; secondly, some of the recommendations are in stark contrast to the requirements of innovation and sometimes contradict each other fundamentally. Intermediaries also suffer from the disadvantage of innovation, which is that nobody has done it before. However, there is a lack of realisation that there is therefore no blueprint for implementation. Rather, everyone fishes in the pond of their own possibilities and the only thing that can be right is what brings commission into the broker's coffers.

To make the dilemma a little more tangible, perhaps this image will help: Imagine you own a leaf frog green Lamborghini with premium equipment that you would like to sell at a fair price. You make use of suitable intermediaries. In other words, people who have successfully sold cars before. The feedback that you receive from potential buyers via the agent is that the numerous potential buyers would like to buy the car from you. It would just have to be yellow and a Porsche. Another agent tells you that it would have to be red and a Ferrari. The real and hard message is: You have the wrong agents. They are not in a position to sell what you have to offer. Instead, they are clear in their demands for commission and blunt in their suggestions for improvement in line with their brokerage success. There is a complete lack of comparison with the benefits of the recommendations for the innovation and the innovator's company. After all, the broker cannot sell otherwise. This means that the money is missing and it is therefore foreseeable that nothing will work out with the innovation. This intermediary triple jump is not only resource-intensive, but often also a heavy burden for the innovator. There is too little that is useful and the recommendations are too far removed from business reality.

But how do you separate the wheat from the chaff? We don't have a patent solution here either. However, a very good approach is to verify the solidity of the broker by asking him about the amount he is going to invest in the company. The polite excuse is often that he is happy to put in some of the commission. However, this obscures the real problem: during the brokerage process, the »critical investor«

will inevitably ask whether and to what extent the broker himself has invested in this unique opportunity. If the wrong answer is given, the brokerage will not be successful. The simple analysis of the »critical investor«: If not even the broker, who claims to be very close to the innovation, invests, why should I invest? Unfortunately, rejection is all too often caused by a lack of commitment on the part of the intermediary rather than by the design of the business model or the innovation itself.

»Retainers« and the desire for a separate travel expense report can also be just as bad faith. Simply calculate the commission in the event of success. You will then realise that both »retainer« and travel expenses must be rounded up to the level of a rounding error. Otherwise, these fees are ridiculous in relation to the commission. The self-assessment of the agent's chances of success is therefore correspondingly low.

Exclusivity is another problem. You should only grant it with the utmost caution. This has something to do with how the agent's day-to-day work is organised after signing the commission conditions. Because the agent often doesn't take any notes at all, he may still make contact with a potential interested party, but the innovator has to take over after that at the latest. After all, he is much better at communicating things and responding to »critical questions«. This is nonsense, because it means that from this point onwards you are doing the agent's job – without him giving you any of his commission in return. That is extremely unsatisfactory. What's more, especially for large companies, the agent will approach anyone with exclusivity – even as a cold contact, because you can't check the quality of the contact – just to be able to pocket the commission on every possible deal from then on.

A clear time limit for the commitment, an iterative review of the learning curve and success and a swift separation in the event of failure are the only instruments left to the innovator in such a mixed situation. Of course, this is difficult. An alternative to this is a clear commitment in communication. Make yourself scarce as soon as you realise that you are employing a time waster. Make sure that this mediator does not spread their wings.

Those who impose themselves as consultants from an intermediary role are a special step up from intermediaries. These are the free riders who make themselves important in your environment and flirt with your innovation and their supposed consultancy mandate. This also includes those who are supposedly sent because a few very shy investors have personally asked them to carry out the on-site review. Free riders are also annoying when they abuse you for free consulting. None of this helps you, uses up your resources and costs you energy. You should turn that off.

What it's all about

Agents promise the moon at the beginning. They do this to get the most far-reaching concessions from you. Disillusionment is usually not long in coming. This is all the more likely the less committed the broker is. You should put a stop to this uncontrolled growth. Reduce commitments of this kind to the minimum possible and consistently monitor their success. You can get a litmus test of the agent's resilience by asking about their own investment in your company. The answer will show you unvarnished where you stand.

It is also advisable to carry out a joint test before a broad »offensive«. Approach an initial contact together to see whether the agent has understood everything that they have not usually noted down anyway. Such »super brains« will approach you again and again with the same questions. Don't be surprised or annoyed, but give them a pen and a notepad instead. This will help them wake up.

You will notice that I am critical of intermediaries. This is because we have learned the hard way that no agent who has not invested in us has ever achieved a single successful placement. That wears you down in the long run, because every briefing, every initial interest raises new hopes that this time it could be different. But it isn't.

The best tool for us was, is and remains communication. Get yourselves talked about in the media, draw attention to yourselves. Then you have a chance of being found.

How to read

»INTERMEDIARIES AND FREE RIDERS«

› What do I employ intermediaries for today?

› What exactly do I need intermediaries for?

› What agreements do they require from me?

› Am I prepared to invest my resources in the intermediaries?

› Do my agents sell what I have to offer at all and competently, or am I being misused by the agents to do their job?

› Which brokers understand my innovation and my business model before they make me promises and set off?

› Do I realise that intermediaries who are not sufficiently enthusiastic about my innovation and who are not convinced by my business model have no chance of success from the outset and are just time wasters?

THE DISAPPOINTMENT IMPACT INVESTOR

What's inside

Impact. This is something every innovator dreams of. Creating a lasting effect. How nice that there are also investors who are committed to doing just that. Impact. They address exactly what we innovators bring to the table. They help us to create this sustainable effect. They are not just backers, but see themselves as part of the idea. Because they share the same goal. At least that's the first impression. However, when it comes to the conditions under which they could get involved, you realise that they are actually no different from those offered by regular investors. This episode is about how to deal with this disappointment and avoid stepping into harm's way.

The episode

We all have some kind of inner drive. We follow an inner plan. Some of us more consciously than others. In any case, the inner drive to make a lasting contribution to the development of the world is often a major driving force behind embarking on the arduous and challenging journey of realising an innovation. So it feels all the better when you meet people who share this perspective among all the investors. People who feel the need to make a contribution to a better world just as much as the innovator themselves. The perspectives complement each other, quickly creating a feeling of inner connection and closeness. A match.

This makes it all the more jarring to realise that the common ground suddenly ends when it comes to financing. Because then it's suddenly all about returns. And it is clear that you can create an impact in many areas: AI, biotech, food and defence are naturally competing with the energy transition for investment funds. Even a well-meaning basic conviction that an energy transition is needed doesn't help. Suddenly there is no longer any common basis for conviction. Only returns. The innovator should be prepared for the fact that an interest rate of up to 15 % per year must be offered for a loan with the risk of an innovation so that investors are prepared to put their own money or that of their background investors on this innovation in the first place. What business case could possibly support such an outrageous interest rate? This brazen demand clearly contradicts the requirement to offer competitive prices. Price leadership is usually the «no brainer« to make it safely into the market. However, if the innovation – due to the start of production – operates beyond the reach of economies of scale and is additionally burdened with this interest burden, then the finite nature of the impact is not far off.

Impact investors see themselves as people who fundamentally want something good, who take their time, who take on risk – and then carry out due diligence, just like any normal investor. Impact quickly becomes a fraudulent label, especially as there are financing instruments that are granted on much more favourable terms. »Soft loans« are instruments that offer an interest rate far below the market average. They are generally intended for developing countries, but are also made available to innovators – if you come across genuine impact investors. For everyone else, I generally claim that they use the impact to have a higher chance of landing with the innovators with their conditions, which are certainly comparable to »normal« investors. To me, this feels like abuse, as such people are playing with my inner conviction and at the same time their audacity is intellectually crassly underchallenging. What chutzpah to assume that people won't see through this ruse?

If you confront such impact investors with the available, significantly more favourable options, the following question puts the cherry on top of the cake: Why would these investors offer on such terms? My view on this: Perhaps because – unlike the current dialogue partner – they are actually interested in an impact. A reply after which the conversation becomes noticeably colder, but which is nevertheless necessary. After all, an agreement corridor for the conditions was not opened anyway.

What it's all about

Impact investors differ from »normal« investors in that they share the conviction that innovations can make a sustainable impact for a better world. This basic conviction combined with the financial strength to finance innovation is a »perfect match« for many innovators.

Caution is advised if this shared conviction is merely the label on the packaging. This can be seen from the fact that the conditions by such supposed impact investors are no different from those imposed by »normal« investors, or are even worse. The term »disappointment« has something to do linguistically with the unmasking of a deception and is a good and important realisation in this context. Nobody needs this deceptive packaging. It is – even if the solidarity of conviction still succeeds – a good reason not to go any further in this direction.

Real impact investors, on the other hand, are those who actually share your convictions. You are not essentially discussing their returns with them. You can openly discuss with them what you need to succeed. Transparency, mutual understanding and trust prevail here – the pillars of a long-term collaboration.

So check carefully whether you are hearing what you really want to hear or whether what you are hearing is a good match for what you need. There is a big difference between the two. If the impact is a fraudulent label, don't bother, because then the rest won't be right either – and you'll be on the hamster wheel of making money for others and therefore miles away from your innovation. Keep your focus, even if you are overwhelmed by the positive feeling that comes from agreeing with your inner drive. Abuse often starts with a candy, don't take it – its too obvious.

How to read

»THE DISAPPOINTMENT IMPACT INVESTOR«

› What is my inner drive?

› What are my core beliefs that others can easily relate to?

› How can I check whether the impact investor is serious?

› Can I compare the conditions of the Impact Investor with those of conventional investors?

› How do I immunise myself against the siren song of the label swindlers?

› How do I make sure that I don't lump every impact investor together?

› Am I prepared to enter into each of these discussions transparently and with the necessary trust, which is the basic prerequisite for any real impact?

YES, NO IPO

What's inside

When start-ups go public, there is regularly a storm of enthusiasm. IPO, or Initial Public Offering, is the shorthand term for going public. Another breakthrough. Another vein of gold that can be mined via the stock exchange. Relief is written all over the founders' faces as they celebrate their first day of trading on the trading floor. After all, this joyous event was preceded by a period of intensive preparation. Blood, sweat and tears. Once it's done, innovation is an almost magical attraction. Nevertheless, the initial enthusiasm all too often turns out to be a flash in the pan. This is because many of these innovations suddenly fall short of investors' expectations. The pressure from the stock market is enormous and sometimes overpowering. There are two sides to this coin: going public and being public. This episode looks at why you should consider this step very carefully and take precautions in good time.

The episode

»When are you planning your IPO?« This is a question that your investors are as sure to ask as the »Amen« in church. But what's it all about? Why do most investors ask it? What does it mean for innovation and for the company? These are the right questions for a critical examination of the IPO topic.

Let's start at the beginning. Before you can even set your sights on an IPO, the innovation must have reached a level of maturity that makes it possible to go public in the first place. Yes, the future is traded on the stock exchange. And yes, the stock market is fundamentally nervous. Even if your idea can have a glorious future, you still have to convince the stock exchange. The idea alone is not enough. Even in the case of SPACs, special purpose acquisition companies, which lack the idea, it is the experienced founders who are trusted to build up a promising portfolio of company investments with the money raised. So, it's all about conviction. Only then does going public have any chance of success.

So, if a lot of homework had to be done before the IPO, it is quite likely that this preparation has already cost a lot. It is equally likely that these necessary investments were made possible by the capital of investors who are naturally interested in their return. This is exactly what the financial side of innovation is all about. An IPO offers early investors the opportunity to significantly increase the value of their shares. Depending on the rules that the company has set itself for the IPO, it also offers the chance to recoup the capital invested in the hype of the IPO by selling own shares and achieving a decent return. With a bit of luck, there will still be enough shares left over to provide an immediate opportunity without any risk. The partial exit of these investors gives them back the freedom to invest in further projects and rewards them with the opportunity from the additional shares gained.

So far, so good. Now the second phase begins: being listed on the stock exchange. This is a completely different league for young companies. There are extensive reporting obligations and regulations that need to be observed. Shareholder management takes centre stage. It's about reaffirming enthusiasm every day so that investors believe in the innovation and the share price continues to rise. Every mistake, every uncertainty is immediately penalised. And that is through a falling share price. This pressure is enormous. It is a high price to pay for satisfying the return interests of your own investors.

That's why it's crucial to know exactly why you want to take your innovation public. After all, the majority of all companies worldwide are not listed on the stock exchange. If you go by the probabilities, going public is therefore more of an exception that needs to be carefully considered. In discussions with investors, however, this reality shifts. It is often suggested that an innovation is only successful if it is linked to an IPO. This is a dangerous hypothesis, as many company developments prove. The unqualified recommendation to go public and the lack of alternatives to an IPO are usually the result of the advisor's interest in a lucrative partial or even complete exit. On the face of it, stock market wisdom is right: no investor has ever gone bankrupt from realised profits.

The future is traded on the stock exchange. These are expectations regarding the potential of innovation and market development in the innovation environment. Let's play it out in concrete terms using our own example. We don't need more than 30 people to develop our technology. Our licensing business model scales with the production of our licensees. We can use this to finance all the activities that we have already planned on our technology development roadmap. So why an IPO? For the sake of this example, let's put this question aside and answer it later. If we went public with this story, after the storm of euphoria we would be compared with other technology developers in the battery sector. They all employ a lot more people and have a lot more money. This raises doubts as to how we intend to hold our own in this environment. The risk perspective is gaining the upper hand. The stock market is losing confidence and withdrawing its trust in us. The result: a price erosion with the risk of degenerating into a penny stock. This is the worst case scenario for every company on the stock market. The end of the story. From that moment on, the innovation has a tag on its toe like a corpse in the coroner's office.

So back to the question of what an IPO is supposed to be useful for. An IPO offers the opportunity to raise capital. It is therefore an alternative financing strategy. Established companies in particular benefit from this by financing new projects through capital increases on shares. However, the story must be so robust that the confidence of the stock market will not be shaken, at least in the medium term. Security is therefore the closest ally of confidence. This is precisely the decisive bottleneck factor for innovations, even at this stage. Don't forget the decisive disadvantage of innovation, namely that nobody has done it before. That's why the IPO itself is by no means a guarantee of success like a ready-made cake. It merely spreads the hope over many more shoulders and redistributes the risks of the original investors – in favour of those who benefit from this step through a partial or complete exit.

In view of our business model, the expected resource requirements and the penny stock risk, we are certain: »Yes, we don't plan an IPO.« We would have almost put this message on the big screen of the NASDAQ in Times Square in New York if a person in charge hadn't taken a closer look. His justification for a full stop of this commercial was a highlight in itself for us: »That would be like Burger King advertising on a McDonald's screen!« We opted for the more conciliatory model of a Christmas tree. A format that was so well received that NASDAQ has already asked us if they could use this idea for other partners.

In contrast to the IPO, our model provides for a consistent high-dividend policy. Due to the scaling with production and the manageable costs for our core business of technology development, we are able to distribute a veritable portion of our annual net profit to shareholders as dividends. This means that even without an IPO, we are one of the stocks that are included in the share portfolio for basic security due to their high dividends. With the subtle difference that our shares cannot be bought on the stock exchange. Due to the limited number of shares and the waiver of capital increases on shares, i.e. the waiver of dilution, the decision to join our shareholder base simply has to be made in good time. We therefore call our shareholder base the HPB Club.

What it's all about

The initial public offering, or IPO for short, is an instrument with a special appeal. Especially from the point of view of the investors who come on board beforehand. After all, it offers the opportunity to recoup one's investment and achieve an attractive return through a partial exit, i.e. a partial sale of one's own shares. And it does so while retaining a residual amount of shares that allows the investor to participate in the opportunity without any further risk.

When assessing the benefits of an IPO for you and your innovation, you should be more far-sighted. After all, an IPO is anything but a guarantee of success, just as your innovation is anything but a ready-made cake. What are the advantages of an IPO for your company and your innovation? Put on blinkers when answering this question. Focus on just this one question. Everything else is completely secondary. Because if it is not advantageous for your company and your innovation, then it is a risk for your success and therefore disadvantageous in your specific case – regardless of what everyone else tries to tell you.

Involve your investors in answering this question. You will get valuable advice from the right investors. Those who are only looking out for their own advantage will realise that they cannot help you answer this question.

How to read

»YES, NO IPO«

› Who is currently driving the idea of an IPO in our company?

› What would be the advantage for our company and our innovation?

› Are we sufficiently sure that we want to and can do this?

› Have we done our homework?

› Do we have the right people on board for this new challenge?

› What does this step mean for all our previous processes?

› What can we gain and what can we lose?

FANTASY OF OMNIPOTENCE VIA BUSINESS MODEL

What's inside

Google, Amazon, Tesla and others are examples of extraordinary entrepreneurial success. The entrepreneurs have become fabulously rich with their companies. They have tremendous influence and enormous creative freedom. That is why they quickly become shining examples. In retrospect, their model of action is obvious and, from today's perspective, there is virtually no alternative. However, this view suggests that such companies were designed on a drawing board right from the start and that all that was needed was to implement this plan consistently. This episode looks at why the business model plays a decisive role.

The episode

The potential of an idea must be quantified sooner or later. Investors and innovators need a framework against which they can orientate themselves. One popular method is the idea of »fair market share«. This idea combines two positive perspectives: on the one hand, the principle »where there is no competition, there is no market« applies. On the other hand, the innovation has the potential to take a share of the current market away from the competition and even expand the market, or even open up new markets. This approach takes you from narrowing down the relevant market to estimating the market volume, which you reduce to the actual addressable market according to your own abilities, from which you then take a share, the »fair market share«, for yourself and your innovation. Not an easy exercise. However, the end result is a number. The level of ambition, the benchmark against which you can align yourself and your activities.

The larger and more significant the innovation, the larger the addressable market and the greater the »fair market share«. At this point at the latest, you should pause and consider what conditions need to be created in order to achieve this »fair market share« in the first place. If it turns out that these conditions cannot realistically be met on their own, it is time to scrutinise the chosen role models, provided they are Google, Amazon, Tesla and the like. Because from this realisation, a continued »solo effort« tips over from opportunity into the category of »omnipotence fantasy«. Trapped in this fantasy, you have unlimited resources at your disposal, everyone around you welcomes your actions and restrictions are just a side note on the timeline. When this house of cards collapses, it becomes unpleasant for everyone involved. Because an open feedback culture has long since been lost along the way.

An alternative to the trap of fantasies of omnipotence is the business model. This is where the opportunities that innovation offers to its promoters should be anchored. In this context, sponsors are the innovators themselves, investors, customers, users and partners who help with the realisation. Let's make it concrete: with our HPB Solid-State Battery, we have an innovation in our hands that can change the world. Created for a sustainable energy and mobility transition. The core characteristics of safer, more durable and greener are a solid foundation for an even more solid »fair market share«. Consequently, we have applied for patents for our HPB Solid-State Electrolyte in 96 countries around the world. If we wanted to realise the potential in the various fields of application and diverse markets on our own, we would have to build up enormous production capacities ourselves. We would need to invest sums that are far beyond our availability. Quite simply, it would be completely unrealistic, at this point in time, to go it alone and thus to pursue a fantasy of omnipotence. It therefore seemed more sensible to us to set up the business model in such a way that we concentrate on what we are very good at: Technology development. Based on this, it made sense to offer our technology by way of licencing to partners who know their own markets and want to develop them with our technology. Partners who can utilise our unique selling points, the much-cited USPs, to improve their own positioning and thus boost our success. Coming from the user side, we have realised that the end customers of our technology will generally not buy their storage system directly from the battery manufacturer.

We have therefore separated the roles of manufacturers and »distributors«, i.e. the sellers to the end customers, and have since differentiated between licences for fields of application and licences for production. In the special case of electromobility, there is a trend towards in-house production by the automotive industry. This is associated with their own battery development. If we want to play a role in this market, we need to focus even more strongly. Because we don't want to develop batteries for the automotive industry, we have derived our third licence area from this: the licence for our HPB Solid-State Electrolyte as a relevant component for the cell development of car manufacturers.

Our business model therefore consistently favours cooperation rather than going it alone. We are very clear and very consistent in this. Things get suspenseful when our business model is »put to the test« by our licensees or prospective licensees. Here we start from scratch again: the fantasy of omnipotence takes hold and tries to hijack our business model through the back door. A special kind of lowlight illustrates this phenomenon and the need for clarity, transparency and consistency. In the context of financing the production of one of our licensees, the first issue was the actual financing of the first production. The more clearly the potential of our technology was understood by the investor, the more extensive the ideas became about what could be realised in the role of licensee. From the franchise model to consulting for other licensees with the obligation to contract through to worldwide exclusivity for wind and solar power buffering. It became more and more gigantic. The capital requirement quickly reached the billions. When it came to checking the contracts for feasibility, proof of capital and a market access strategy in addition to an adequate commitment, we fell out of favour just as quickly as our technology had led to fantasies of omnipotence.

Such a development of the discussion is not favourable for the implementation of an innovation. The capital requirement very quickly becomes so high that a short-term start becomes increasingly difficult, the associated contracts increasingly complex and the consumption of resources in the initiation process increasingly sprawling. At the end of the day, such developments are simply not realisable. The tangible start is missing. The start of a shared journey. Time and again, we are faced with the discussion that we need to organise the implementation of technology as a group. As a network of majority shareholdings that would allow us to get much more out of the technology for our shareholders. This discussion regularly fails to recognise that the establishment of battery production facilities worldwide is associated with enormous costs. These funds would have to be raised on the capital market. Extensive reporting obligations would have to be fulfilled, and one would be exposed to the free play of forces on the stock market. At the end of the day, instead of better market development in the interests of shareholders, there would be a large cluster risk. The fatal idea behind this is that you can do everything on your own and, above all, better than others. Just like the great role models show us. Omnipotence fantasy »at its best«.

What it's all about

»*Ex post*«, i.e. with hindsight, everyone would have done the same as the super successful entrepreneurs behind Google,

Amazon, Tesla and co. »*Ex ante*«, i.e. from today into the future, it's a random game of chance. Because an innovation develops over time. It grows with its challenges and new opportunities and risks open up every day. If the level of ambition is overstretched, it becomes difficult to even come close to realising it. Instead, pressure and stress increase and the initial good spirit of the start-up and innovation is lost.

It doesn't have to come to that. If, despite all the euphoria about the enormous opportunities of your own innovation, you pause for a moment and ask yourself how exactly this really big wheel should be turned, then you will realise that the nut may still be too hard to crack. Then it's time to review your own business model. Is it easier? Is it beneficial to change the design of the business model? Is it expedient to pool resources with partners and overcome restrictions? These are questions that will help you to anchor the necessary clarity in your business model. This clarity makes you immune to external fantasies of omnipotence. Attracting the right investors is hard enough. However, fending off fantasies of omnipotence becomes increasingly troublesome over time. Unmask fantasies of omnipotence by translating them into short-term operational reality together with the idea provider. You will see how beneficial this excursion will be in the short term if they do not have the necessary financial resources. Then you still have the option of entering into a completely normal collaboration for mutual benefit. And without resorting to fantasies of omnipotence.

How to read

»FANTASY OF OMNIPOTENCE OVER BUSINESS MODEL«

› How »immeasurably large« does my »fair market share« appear?

› How much does my innovation inspire my partners' thoughts in terms of »fantasies of omnipotence«?

› How convinced am I that I can do everything better on my own?

› Do I have sufficient resources to realise my innovation on my own?

› Apart from the »immeasurable« opportunities, what risks arise from the path of self-realisation of all potentials?

› How can I immunise myself, my innovation and my business model against the »hostile takeover« by fantasies of omnipotence?

› What do I gain if I divide the potential of my idea between different independent partners?

THE DIRTY BUSINESS OF SUBSIDIES

What's inside

Sponsorship is a privilege. It is external support on particularly favourable terms. There are private sponsors and the public sector, i.e. support from the state and therefore ultimately from the taxpayer. Private sponsors cover a broad spectrum of support, this ranges from coaching and networking to financial support. Each sponsor sets its own rules here. Such sponsors differ from investors in that their inner motivation is more complex than their own financial gain. Public funding, on the other hand, appears to be a cornucopia of financial resources that are distributed according to clear and transparent rules. This episode is about a reality check for this ideal.

The episode

In principle, public funding is provided where other means are not or not yet available. It is intended to close a gap that many ideas and innovations would otherwise not be able to overcome on their own due to a lack of established economic interest. The spectrum is huge. There is public funding for almost every idea. This »economic sector« is correspondingly huge. Particularly in the area of public funding, there are countless institutions and service providers that live from funding. It's about the distribution of billions – every year.

In Germany, there is a kind of basic need, namely the need for rules. Without rules, everything leads to chaos. With rules, everything is transparent and comprehensible for everyone. This is also the guiding principle behind public funding. The entire process of allocating funds is correspondingly complex: so-called funding guidelines provide the basic framework. These regulate which projects can be funded, under what conditions and to what extent. The applicant then first submits a funding outline, which is assessed by independent experts. There is usually an evaluation matrix for this evaluation, which leads to a score value. In this way, the individual projects are sorted and prioritised if the available funding volume is oversubscribed. If the evaluation is positive, the applicant is invited to submit the actual funding application. This is also analysed and evaluated in detail. Because both the special language of the funding guidelines and the art of submitting an application represent an arbitrary hurdle for many innovators, numerous experts offer their services in the field of funding acquisition. Many of these even work on a success basis. In some cases, the consultancy support itself can be subsidised.

This is the translation of the guiding principle of transparency and traceability of public funding in Germany. In principle, the same funding rules for the public sector apply in Europe. It would only be possible to compare the extent to which the concrete organisation is regulated to a similar extent if the funding conditions for a given project could be compared concretely and country-specifically. However, this idea fails because, in order to be eligible for funding in principle, a company must also be based in the country in which funding is applied for. Projects that pursue an overarching European goal therefore rely on cooperation. These are projects in which several partners from different European countries join forces to realise a project together.

There may be a gradient of funding complexity if you draw the line from niche applications to key technologies. With our battery innovation, we are certainly located in the area of key technologies. These are technologies that are of decisive importance for the development of society as a whole and for the national economy. Batteries are not only important for the mobility transition towards electromobility, but are also of crucial importance in the energy transition when it comes to balancing electricity generation and consumption. The market is currently dominated by China. The Chinese have recognised how important this key technology is for the global economy. Consequently, this is exactly where their strategy of dominance comes in. In Europe, on the other hand, we are finding it extremely difficult to successfully establish our own battery production. We are in danger of being left behind. This topic has been receiving corresponding attention in the area of public funding for some time now.

We have already tried to access such subsidies with the

first subsidy package from Federal Economics Minister Altmaier. Without success. We know that our technology was one of eight consortia that applied for the billions in funding. We have not even received a confirmation of receipt. We then applied to the »Reallabore der Energiewende«, e. g. real-world laboratories for the energy transition and other funding formats. However, we never got beyond the funding outline stage. We have since learnt that there are some good reasons for this. These are not necessarily representative of the entire funding landscape. However, for me at least, they raise questions as to whether they even begin to do justice to the guiding principle of transparent and comprehensible funding for projects that would have no chance of development without funding.

The first hurdle is the lack of expertise and individual sensitivities on the part of the evaluators. In our case, we are regularly told that what we are presenting is too good to be true. Highly decorated chemists who are initially enthusiastic about the new possibilities quickly realise that a real solution to the issues of the energy and mobility transition is not wanted at all. On the contrary: behind closed doors, we have learnt that our technology is associated with the risk that other projects that are currently being funded could become superfluous, that previous decisions could be misinterpreted and thus become a reputational risk. Accordingly, we are consistently rejected. The reasons for the rejection are by no means transparent and comprehensible. On the contrary. In fact, the content is incorrect and contestable. We once systematically scrutinised one of these rejections. For the representative of the project organiser, this was certainly one of the toughest rounds he had ever experienced. He responded to our final question about which legal options he would recommend to us with the statement that we could sue our way into the application, but that would then certainly be rejected again. We should simply accept the fact that our technology is not wanted.

We only realised another hurdle later. It is not transparent either, but its consequences are all the more far-reaching. The Taxpayers' Association appears to have a key figure for funding efficiency by which the project organisers must be measured – the administration ratio. It sets the costs of awarding funding in relation to the amount of funding allocated. The lower the ratio, the more efficient the allocation of funds. At first glance, this seems plausible. But at second glance it is fatal. After all, the administrative costs on the part of the project organisers do not vary depending on the funding volume applied for, but rather on the number of projects. This systematically favours large projects over smaller ones and thus fundamentally contradicts the actual purpose of the funding, namely the funding of projects that are not yet mature enough to be supported by other sources.

Finally, a third hurdle lies in the constructed dependency between funding and personal contribution. In the non-university context, the granting of funding requires personal contribution. This personal contribution must be proven before the funding is approved, as otherwise the basic eligibility for funding is not given. This requirement is an almost insurmountable hurdle, especially for start-ups. Investors and banks, who would in principle be prepared to support the project with the necessary financial resources, make this support conditional on funding. After all, the capital required for realisation without funding would be significantly higher and the desired step would not be achievable without the funding. And it is precisely this reservation that does not count as proof of personal contribution. So, such projects are ruled out in the application phase for precisely this reason.

It is striking that spin-offs from the university sector are obviously favoured. On the one hand, this is due to the fact that 100 % funding is standard in the bosom of the alma mater, meaning that projects can be developed for a long time without the university's own contribution. On the other hand, it is, of course, proof of the thrust of the funding when innovations from the university sector in particular find their way into practice. How good that the reviewers come from the same background. At this point, it is important for me to emphasise that I am by no means casting general suspicion on funding. Nor do I want to offend the numerous experts who have an enormous amount of work to do with all the applications and who act to the best of their knowledge and belief. However, I would like to take the liberty of questioning the funding system in its current structure.

In the key battery industry, this structural imbalance means that large projects aimed at setting up gigafactories based on conventional technologies are systematically favoured over genuine innovations. This cements the role of the follower and prevents a return to innovation leadership. This systemic problem is exacerbated by the fact that numerous research institutions in Germany are dependent on research funding. Their path to funding also leads via project applications for funding, thereby increasing the pressure on the system as a whole. And the experts for technology assessment come from precisely these areas. If you come into this process from the non-university sector and without an established brand, the combination of hurdles becomes almost insurmountable. The interests of the actors involved are too complex, the egoisms in deciding on the best use of funds too great. It is even completely irrelevant what evidence can be thrown into the ring from a neutral side for the assessment. It cannot be what must not be. All of this is justified by a transparent and comprehensible process that does not disadvantage anyone and offers a fair chance for everyone. Unfortunately, in practice, at least based on our experience over the last few years and under various governments, the opposite is the case.

Finally, it is worth asking how it is compatible with the principles of subsidisation that companies in the automotive industry, for example, can regularly raise billions in subsidies and at the same time distribute dividends to their shareholders. In these cases, is it really taxpayers' money that motivates a company to invest in its own innovation leadership and thus future viability, or are subsidies used as a welcome opportunity to maximise profits? The latter, at least, cannot be in the interests of the taxpayer. But who am I to question such a hub for billions and even from the sidelines.

What it's all about

Applying for funding is a complicated business. It costs you a huge amount of time and energy. You should therefore seek support from people who understand this business. On the other hand, you should scrutinise exactly what prospects of success you have with your innovation. Who has an interest in your success and who has an interest in your failure? An obviously relevant question is the amount of funding requested. If it is too small, you will be rejected anyway. For the right project size however, you need the necessary equity. Who can provide you with the foundation for brand visibility? And what price do you have to pay for it?

Funding is a privilege. But it is not an end in itself. There are conditions attached to the individual funding programmes that you need to check carefully in advance. For example, the »Bundesagentur für Sprunginnovationen«, i. e. federal agency for leap innovations in Germany, SPRIND, initially had the requirement, based on a birth defect in the European context, that all resulting property rights would accrue to SPRIND. For us as a technology developer with a licensing business model, this is an immediate red light for the elementary »Freedom to Operate« (FTO), i.e. the possibility of being able to grant licences without conflicting with third-party property rights. In other funding contexts, for example, there are conditions that make publication of the results mandatory. These are also conditions whose acceptance you should check in advance.

Incidentally, you are a welcome partner in the area of collaborations with universities and scientific institutions if you can offer a pure industry commission. Here, the rules of the game and the rights are clearly defined in your favour from the outset and business is easier for everyone involved. It is therefore essential that you first consider the advantages and disadvantages of funding for your innovation. Only then should you enter this ostensibly transparent and comprehensible minefield of funding in Germany.

How to read

»THE DIRTY BUSINESS OF SUBSIDIES«

› What specific goals do I associate with public funding?

› How can I ensure that I am neither too small nor too big for the respective funding programme?

› Who can support me with a strong brand to increase my allocation prospects?

› What price am I prepared to pay for the support?

› Do I have a suitable partner with fair conditions for the application?

› Can I actually fulfil the conditions of the grant in the event of a positive funding decision?

› Do I know the consequences of the opportunities and risks from funding for my innovation in detail?

LOBBYING – THE GAME OF THE PRESERVATIONISTS

What's inside

In a parliamentary democracy, the representatives of the people are elected in elections. During the subsequent legislative period, these elected representatives are responsible for legislation and thus hold the levers for the framework conditions for the social and economic interaction of all stakeholders. Regardless of how passionately the education levels of the elected representatives are discussed at the German regulars' tables, it is almost impossible for a politician to be so well versed in all topics that, even from a neutral point of view, their framework specifications are good for the development of the country. Lobbyists are stepping in to close these knowledge gaps. This episode looks at why this is a problem for innovation.

The episode

The clamour about the level of education of our elected representatives is enormous. The regulars' tables in Germany in particular are a great place to badmouth. This completely ignores the fact that, for example, after a record high of 736 MPs in the Bundestag since the electoral law reform of 2023, »only« 630 MPs will be responsible for legislation in the Bundestag in future. Anyone who can claim to have the necessary expertise in all topics that may be affected by the legislative process – regardless of their level of education – should grab one of these 630 seats and help shape our country. For everyone else, it can be assumed that there is a need for »extra tuition« in one area or another. Incidentally, a doctorate in no way protects against this need.

The »tutoring« of politicians takes many forms. One important form is lobbying. This is the representation of interests vis-à-vis politicians in an attempt to exert influence on the legislative process. Despite the supposed transparency of the 27,000 lobbyists now registered with the Bundestag alone, this business is completely opaque. That's an average of 42 lobbyists per MP. Even if, since the novel »The Hitchhiker's Guide to the Galaxy«, 42 is the answer to the »ultimate question of life, the universe and all the rest«, the »tutoring pressure« on politicians is undoubtedly already enormous in the Bundestag. This does not even include the other political levels of the legislature.

On the one hand, this »tutoring pressure« certainly closes the supposedly underlying knowledge gap among politicians in many cases. However – and this is where lobbying differs from tutoring in maths – the legislative response to a given need for regulation is by no means unambiguous. So there is not just »right« and »wrong«, »zero« and »one«. There is a wealth of different perspectives and regulatory options for every regulatory need. The basis of every conflict of interest. It is therefore a necessary part of the special role of lobbying that successful lobbyists not only close a knowledge gap »neutrally«, but can and, wherever possible, do actively co-determine the perspective of the solution. They can literally dictate their version of the regulation to politicians and thus assert their interests over other interests on the same topic.

The success of lobbying is also causally linked to the amount invested by the respective interest group. It is interesting to see which sectors the lobbyists with the largest budgets come from: Banks, insurance companies and investment companies top this list, followed by the car lobby and the chemicals lobby. According to ZDF, their expenditure on maintaining contacts and trying to influence politics alone total around €79 million. This corresponds to a »tutoring budget« of around €125,000 per MP.

However, these figures are not about the numbers themselves. Rather, it is about being aware that although, according to the basic principle of a parliamentary democracy, all power comes from the people, in the actual political opinion-forming process this is tilted in favour of a few. Due to the enormous »tutoring pressure« on politicians and the imbalance in the financial resources between the interest representatives, lobbying harbours the risk that framework conditions are set by politicians which, from a neutral point of view – in the sense of a closed knowledge gap – are not in the interests of the people and the development of the country, but in the interests of the most powerful interest group.

Three simple examples illustrate the basic problem of a

lobbying slate: The regulation that screw caps on plastic bottles or tetrapacks must remain firmly attached to the bottle or tetrapack is a stroke of genius by an interest group and lacks any neutral sense. The requirement to shrink-wrap organic cucumbers in plastic on the grounds of food hygiene was completely overregulated and stood in stark contrast to a more environmentally conscious lifestyle. It used to be enough to wash vegetables before preparing and eating them. Today, we are choking on ever larger mountains of rubbish – partly due to the ingenuity of the packaging industry and its influence on the legislative process. The new regulation of driving licence categories with the division into countless sub-categories essentially only has the consequence for consumers that obtaining a driving licence is becoming ever more expensive. Increased safety or even a reduction in accidents is in no way causally linked to this. With this lobbying pressure, we do not need to complain about excessive bureaucracy or even call for politicians to reduce bureaucracy. After all, every lobbyist wants to see their interests enshrined in law – if only for the sake of planning security.

But what does all this have to do with innovation? Lobbyists represent the interests of their clients. If certain developments are perceived as a threat, they are countered accordingly. Innovation fundamentally harbours the risk of questioning an established »*status quo*«, shaking up established value chains, bringing new players onto the playing field and shifting the balance of power. Innovation thus becomes a risk for those who can »afford« to shape the framework conditions today, for those who can secure their sinecures through their influence. Those who have a lot can exert influence. But those who have a lot today also have a lot to lose tomorrow. Lobbying is a powerful opponent of innovation, and all the more powerful the more innovation could shake up established structures.

As lobbying takes place in the backrooms of politics despite all efforts to achieve transparency, innovations must go on a transparency offensive. A transparency offensive as a »fact-based information offer« to close a knowledge gap that actually exists. Thankfully, there are also enough members of parliament who gain direct access to different perspectives from the people through appropriate citizen participation. In this context, for example, we were invited by the Federal Association for Electromobility (Bundesverband für Elektromobilität, BEM) to take part in a parliamentary dialogue in the Bundestag on the subject of electromobility. It is amazing what effect striking examples can have that are in clear contrast to the dominant perspective. The discussion about charging infrastructure for electric cars in Germany, for example, is dominated by the »grid-centric« expansion concept: every charging point is connected directly to the power grid without a buffer. This makes about as much sense as connecting all petrol pumps at conventional filling stations directly to the oil refinery. All petrol stations have always worked with buffer storage tanks – floor tanks from which the petrol pumps pump the fuel into the tank at high pressure, thus enabling a high level of »charging convenience«. Without the integration of buffer storage tanks into the charging infrastructure, the current expansion idea is a high-risk economic gamble. Whether this realisation will prevail also depends on how consistently this knowledge transfer is repeated. This is precisely where the dependence on financial resources for the necessary knowledge transfer on the part of innovation and innovators comes full circle.

What it's all about

Lobbying is a game of the strongest. Innovation is systematically at a disadvantage here unless it is in the lobbyists' own interests. For you and your innovation, this realisation means that on the one hand you can make an effort to be perceived as advantageous by the lobbyists relevant to your innovation. On the other hand, you can endeavour to create transparency about your innovation environment through media and direct communication with members of parliament.

This is no easy task. After all, it involves a considerable amount of effort – both in terms of time and money. However, if you realise that there is an imbalance in the political decision-making process that is systematically hindering your innovation, you need to »invest« in this field. It helps to familiarise yourself with the mechanisms and rules of interest representation and lobbying and to find the right contacts and strategies in conjunction with your media activities. You will realise that it is also a blessing for politicians to talk to ordinary people who are working as entrepreneurs to bring about change for the good of society, the economy and the environment.

Lobbying is the preservers' game because they have the necessary resources for effective lobbying. Lobbying can therefore be a powerful opponent of your innovation. However, it is worth trying to make your »tutoring offer« to this group as well. The good thing about innovation is that you can only win as long as the innovation has not yet become established. However, you should already have one thought in your mind: If you have achieved a breakthrough with your innovation, then help other innovators with their breakthrough. Don't forget your fight for your innovation and all the efforts associated with it. Otherwise, with your success, you will gradually switch over to the side of the preservationists who are making life so difficult for you today. That would be a disservice to the prosperity-oriented development of our economy and society. A changed self-image in this sense is also innovation.

How to read

»LOBBYISM – THE GAME OF THE PRESERVATIONISTS«

› What are the »big lines« that define my innovation environment today?

› What misunderstandings are causing these lines to stand in the way of my innovation?

› Who benefits from my innovation and who could be negatively affected by my innovation?

› What is the balance of power between the beneficiaries and the disadvantaged of my innovation?

› Which formats of direct and indirect interest representation can I use for my innovation?

› How do I combine my marketing and media activities with the necessary representation of interests?

› How can I help other innovators?

THE HOUSE BANK PRINCIPLE

What's inside

Banks are systemically important. This is their claim and their fundamental function. They are the hub for all electronic financial transactions and the interface between the state, the financial sector and the real economy. They grant loans and manage financial assets via their accounts. In short, they are of crucial importance for companies. This is also the justification for extensive rescue packages when banks have exposed themselves to risks that they are unable to bear in the real economy. However, this episode looks at whether banks live up to the self-perception of systemic importance and what this can mean for innovation.

The episode

In the past, training as a bank clerk was considered the ultimate way to start a promising career. There was a good relationship between bank employees and their customers. Many challenges could be solved through the short channels of communication. But those days are over. Globalisation and the increasing digitalisation of the financial industry have been eroding regional structures for years. Former flexibilities have fallen victim to regulation to prevent further financial crises. The enormous duration of the low interest rate policy has also had a massive impact on the financial sector in all areas. All that remains is the cliché of the banker spoilt by success from the 1990s: Short-sleeved shirt with no vest, Mickey Mouse tie and a gold tie bar in a sleek sports car shape. As outdated as this cliché may seem, it accurately describes how banks deal with the »monster« of innovation.

In principle, three categories are available for financing innovations: Equity, debt and subsidies. Banks have different roles and functions in these three categories. When it comes to the transfer of equity capital, the banks are generally responsible for verifying the origin of the funds. Before relevant deposits are credited to the business account, the banks must ensure that the funds are free of criminal origin. There are international rules in place to prevent money laundering and terrorist financing. If the money checked in this way is clean, it can generally be used. Debt capital can be provided in various ways. As a rule, this involves adequate collateralisation and an interest payment depending on the risk associated with the loan disbursement. The house bank also plays a key role in the allocation of funding. After all, it forwards a loan request for preferential conditions to the Kreditanstalt für Wiederaufbau, or KfW for short. This is a bank through which the German state handles a large part of its subsidy programmes. The role of the house bank here is to carry out the preliminary assessment and the accompanying administration. So far, so good.

However, the »monster« of innovation has the potential to cause considerable turmoil for banks. Especially when the business of innovation is internationally orientated. We have had so many experiences with banks that this topic could fill a book of its own. Nevertheless, I think it would be useful to provide a summarised overview here to spare you the pitfalls we have already stumbled across.

We start this never-ending story on a small scale: The overdraft facility. This is a fundamentally expensive but flexible credit line that helps to bridge outgoing and incoming payments at short notice. Start-ups, including us, are not granted this credit line. This has already led to us being denied this flexibility despite clarifying in advance by telephone whether the social security contributions could be debited if the required funds were credited to the account on the same day. The money arrived in the account on the day of the direct debit as announced. Nevertheless, the debit of the contributions was rejected by the bank. Late payment surcharges and a lot of additional work followed. Another instrument with a relevant flexibility effect is the »Sale & Lease Back« model. Expensive machines, such as a laser welding machine in our case, can usually be purchased by the company first, with the machine being collateralised, and then sold to a bank or leasing partner and leased back by them. This helps to conserve liquidity. Such an instrument is generally not available to innovators who do not yet generate their own sales and instead demonstrably cover their capital requirements with equity – i.e. with the help of investments. The ability to service debt is not given by the balance sheet, which is why overdraft facilities and leasing are structurally excluded.

A positive assessment by the house bank is a mandatory prerequisite for access to favourable loans. However, the bank has insufficient incentives to deal with the assessment of the project in the required form. The processing fee that the bank is allowed to charge KfW seems too low. Accordingly, the time and effort involved in the review seems disproportionate to the loan officers. In addition, the clerks have to check and assess the three risk categories – technology, production and market risk. A small practical test: a bank clerk should therefore be able to assess the project of a solid-state battery with regard to technology, production and market risks? Without wishing to offend the bank employees: They are bank employees because they are looking for a secure job, are generally risk-averse by nature and simply do not see themselves in an entrepreneurial role. They therefore lack the basic prerequisites to fulfil this task. As a result, this audit is reduced to a question of faith in the area of conflict between unattractive remuneration from a banking perspective and the lack of audit skills. Sentences such as »With the best will in the world, I can't imagine that your innovation will succeed« are the rule rather than the exception. The path to KfW's favourable loan conditions is thus blocked. The only supposed solution here: A change of house bank.

The matter becomes problematic when it comes to a loan collateralised by a guarantee. One of our licence holders has received an offer of a stand-by letter of credit (SBLC), a bank guarantee from an investor. With this bank guarantee, one bank guarantees another bank that it will fully assume the risk of loan default over a corresponding period of time. The »excuse« here: »A bank must not only focus on the collateral. It's also about reviewing the technology and the business model.« And here, too, we are caught in the trap of the balancing act between mandate and capabilities. At best, the model is still praised as »unusual«, but in any case, a loan offer with the same term as the bank guarantee is rejected. Incidentally, this attitude runs right through the hierarchy of banks – from the »house bank« to the »Landesbank«. The fact that other battery projects – such as Northvolt – are failing is a particular problem for us and our innovation. These projects are used to assess all three risk categories as significant – regardless of the evidence presented in favour of the superiority of our technology. Above all, it is incomprehensible why projects such as Northvolt have received financial support from banks, which we are systematically denied.

However, the role of European banks becomes downright bizarre when the business model is internationally orientated. Swiss banks belong in the same category in this context. We have applied for patents for our invention in 96 countries. This allows us to roll out our licensing business model worldwide. We do this from Germany and tax all our income in Germany. However, if payments are received from a country outside Europe, we are summarily refused payment and the business relationship is cancelled. The international rules on money laundering checks and the prevention of terrorist financing are suddenly completely irrelevant. The check is not even initiated. The fear of »bad« money from outside Europe is too great in the banking world.

However, if you look at the prospects of success of innovation financing in Europe in an international comparison, you realise that the availability of funds in Europe is anything but satisfactory. On the contrary: many innovations simply have no chance if they rely on funding in Europe. This is why many innovators are moving away from Europe. The few »crazy« entrepreneurs who still want to make it in Europe inevitably have to look outside Europe for funding. Current hubs for innovation financing: China, the USA and the Arab world. Considerable financial resources are available there for the promotion of innovation. However, there is actually no willingness on the part of the European banking world to even begin to provide support here. As a result, the supposedly systemically relevant banks in Europe are literally digging the water out of the equally systemically relevant culture of innovation. How exactly are we supposed to secure our prosperity in Europe if such obstacles are placed in the way of innovation financing? Who is supposed to cushion the future missteps of the banks through their speculation if prosperity erodes? The reference to banking regulation is a cheeky excuse for many of these positions and yet it is justified in principle. It is time to scrutinise the impact of regulation in Europe with a view to preventing innovation. At the same time, however, it is also time for banks to use their undisputed discretionary powers for innovation and in favour of innovators. Without adequate support for innovation financing, there is no innovation, without innovation there is no prosperity and without prosperity there is no bright future. We are certainly not an isolated case.

What it' all about

Banks are risk-averse when it comes to financing innovations. The situation is different when it comes to the creativity of financial instruments. Asset management plays in a completely different league with its risk instruments and leverage products. And the banks earn easy money with them. If the banks are given the role of evaluating innovations, the buck stops with the »small minds«. Neither the personality profile nor the skillset of the average banker includes the ability to evaluate innovations or weigh up their opportunities and risks. The risk-averse view of the »monster« of innovation dominates. This gives the impression that you are doing your bank a disservice if you approach them with your own innovation and need for support. The excuses range from flimsy to downright cheeky, the support tends towards zero. At least from the point of view of innovation, this is a memorable role for so-called systemically important banks.

But what does this mean for you and your innovation? You need to familiarise yourself in good time with the fact that your choice of bank can pose a fatal risk to your innovation. This ranges from the refusal of flexible liquidity support to the unilateral cancellation of the business relationship as soon as sales from a non-European country are announced. It is important to anticipate these risks. We have addressed the issue of trusteeship. We have learnt that it is not enough to be vehement advocates of preventing money laundering and combating the financing of terrorism and to make a commitment to Germany as a business location, including accepting the relatively high tax burden. The majority of banks in Europe simply do not care about these points.

It is about nothing less than a future-proof organisation

of an international banking cooperation that enables you to roll out your innovation worldwide and earn honest money with it. The house bank principle in Europe is not only a risk for your innovation on a small scale, but above all for scaling. Tackle this problem in good time. It won't help you to postpone solving these issues – the cancellation of the business relationship by your house bank will not prevent this. And in case of doubt, this will hit you faster than you would like.

How to read

»THE HOUSE BANK PRINCIPLE«

› Am I in good hands with my bank today when it comes to liquidity support and access to financing?

› How international is my business model?

› From which countries do I expect sales or investments?

› What is my bank's position on this?

› What does my bank carry, where does it get out?

› How do I compensate for my bank's shortcomings by working with trustees and international banks?

› What implications does this have for my business model?

THE ROLE OF POLITICS

What's inside

The state has an important function for social cohesion. The principle of the separation of powers in Germany is enshrined in Article 20 (2) sentence 2 of the Basic Law. The state ensures legislation through the legislative branch and thus creates the framework for coexistence. It implements these norms through the executive. Through the judiciary, it sanctions misconduct across all levels and hierarchies. Tax money is used to organise the welfare state and create and maintain public infrastructures. There is only one role that the state does not fulfil in its pure form: the role of the entrepreneur. Nevertheless, since the financial crisis, the feeling has been creeping in more and more that the state must participate in the risk-taking of the economy. Systemic relevance is the key buzzword here. Why this is particularly dangerous for innovation is the subject of this episode.

The episode

All power comes from the people. Elections are held to elect the people's representatives, who then enact laws within the framework of the separation of powers, enforce them and sanction misconduct. Politics therefore has the task of setting and enforcing the framework for social interaction. Politics therefore sets the framework conditions.

Since the financial crisis triggered by the collapse of Lehman Bank – also known as »the bank of evil« in the animated film »Despicable Me« – the term »systemic importance« has become part of common parlance. The effects of the Lehman bankruptcy were so fundamental, the proliferation of financial instruments so considerable and the interrelationships between the banks so extensive that the entire global economy was thrown into turmoil. Without further ado, billions were spent to prevent a gigantic wave of bank failures as collateral damage of the Lehman bankruptcy. Since then, it seems to have become good form to invoke systemic relevance in order to collectivise risks, i.e. to pass them on to the taxpayer, and to individualise profits, i.e. to pass them on to shareholders. The automotive industry also regularly claims to be the central key industry in Germany and therefore systemically relevant to a certain extent. Every time there is a market shock, there are calls for scrappage incentives and other models to promote sales and thus prevent major job losses. The problem with this approach is that these measures generally have a short-term effect and make the state increasingly vulnerable to blackmail. Often played off against each other: Jobs and innovation.

The energy crisis has uncovered another phenomenon: when the gas was turned off, energy prices in Germany shot through the roof. Electricity price brakes and petrol price brakes became the saviours of relief for the downtrodden citizens. Profits at the major energy companies also shot through the roof. This was followed by considerable inflation, as the increased energy prices were passed on to consumers via the products. This was followed by wage adjustments, which further fuelled and cemented the inflation rate. And all this despite the fact that the commodity markets had eased considerably within a relatively short period of time. However, this was not utilised in anything like the same proportion to lower prices as the rise in prices for all products had been justified shortly before. It was only this spiral that turned a short-term price effect into a sustainable inflation effect. After all, people are not earning more money, but the money is worth less. A good example of this is buying a house: if you buy a house, don't invest and sell it ten years later at twice the price, the price increase cannot be attributed to value-enhancing measures. What remains is speculation and real inflation. The money is only worth half as much ten years later – if you ignore speculation effects.

Since the financial crisis at the latest, the state has started to solve economic problems with billions in taxes. In the good faith that this would prevent far worse problems. However, the examples of the electricity price brake and the petrol price brake clearly show that these billions in taxes have not changed the root causes of the symptoms. On the contrary: the symptoms got worse and worse, precisely because the root causes were not addressed. Incidentally, this is by no means a party-specific problem. It is a creeping departure from the original tasks of the state. The more successful it is to transfer the risks of economic trade to the state using bogus arguments such as systemic relevance and job security, the easier it is to operate from an entrepreneurial perspective. This is particularly dangerous for innovations because innovators generally have much less access to these instruments and to influencing political decisions.

If, on the other hand, one looks at the energy crisis from a framework perspective, there would have been the possibility of changing the pricing mechanism in addition to an electricity price brake. With this mechanism, the highest price of the base load determines the electricity price. If an energy source that is price-relevant in this context is taken »hostage« by a shortage, the price explosion is anchored in the current pricing mechanism. If electricity generation from gas had been removed from this mechanism and only this component had been subsidised by the state, electricity prices would probably not have shown this price explosion. This example is not about concrete quantification. Rather, it is about qualifying the scope of options arising from the original area of political responsibility: The framework legislative competence. The electricity price brake has only superficially lowered the electricity price for consumers, as the price difference to the »market price« was compensated by the state – and thus in turn by the taxpayer – vis-à-vis the energy companies. The same applies to the petrol price brake. Where are the cartel authorities when it comes to this kind of rip-off, where are the politicians when it comes to stopping such uncontrolled growth, such unbridled self-service by a few?

The hopelessness of politics in reactive mode seems plausible if one assumes that action must be taken quickly in order not to lose the favour of voters. Fiscal relief with a watering can also saves a necessary and probably complex reorganisation of the regulations. Too many interests are involved here, too many dependencies now exist between politics and business.

In terms of supporting innovation, politicians are now increasingly and publicly calling for the provision of guarantees to favour private-sector financing of innovation. €50 million here, €600 million there. Those who demand this are asking for nothing less than the state to take on an entrepreneurial role. It would be much more expedient for the state to concentrate on the framework conditions. For the energy transition to be successful in the long term, it absolutely needs storage facilities because generation and consumption often diverge. The term »Dunkelflaute«, i. e. «dark doldrums» has even become internationally famous. However, instead of improving the framework conditions for the use of storage systems, individual projects are being subsidised with considerable funds. For example, the battery production of Northvolt. The public sector has provided over €600 million in guarantees. An assumption of risk for a single commercial enterprise. Money that is lacking for the fulfilment of original and sovereign tasks of the state. Money that is not granted to other innovators in the battery industry in Germany. The refusal of a €50 million guarantee for Lilium, an air taxi company, has triggered a veritable shitstorm among politicians. From my entrepreneurial point of view, this is an absolutely wrong development – also on the part of entrepreneurs and investors who vehemently demand this role of the state.

It is impossible for the state to guarantee every company. There is therefore a risk of considerable distortion of competition for the industry concerned. It would be interesting to know whether the private investors bear comparable risks by granting a guarantee, as the state is supposed to assume through the guarantee. The guarantee for Northvolt at least suggests this question.

It's nice when the state wants to play entrepreneur. It's also a great way to show off to your colleagues. After all, you're not gambling with your own money, but only with that of the taxpayers. Of course, there are examples where things have gone well. The partial nationalisation of Lufthansa is one such example. The state made a total profit of €760 million on its exit in 2022. In my opinion, however, we are increasingly losing sight of what politics is actually there for, namely the framework conditions for social cohesion and cooperation.

For future-oriented development, politics must return to its traditional role and focus on the framework conditions. This has a much broader impact, especially for innovations. The following applies: »less is more« and »quality before speed«. Just how important it is to review the incentivising effect of the framework conditions can be seen, for example, in the regulations on the recycling quota for battery raw materials. With an exponential increase in demand, an increase in recycling rates can only be guaranteed through short-life batteries and high scrap rates – in short, through poor technology. As a result, this leads to more resource consumption and is therefore counterproductive to the well-intentioned regulatory interest.

Politics, on the other hand, offers a special and extremely valuable advantage in the area of networking. Due to their necessary proximity to voters, politicians are generally very well networked. Their offices open doors to levels that innovators would often find difficult to access without a network. This type of networking is an important contribution by politicians to the development of innovations. Coupled with a focus on framework conditions, politics can support innovation with much less risk and in the necessary breadth than is even possible with billions in tax revenue and risk-taking.

What it's all about

Politics creates the framework conditions. Politicians are often well connected. Both factors are important for your innovation. You can endeavour to make your points of view and your need for framework conditions transparent to the relevant authorities. You can also persuade politicians to open doors for you through their network where it will help your innovation.

In the true entrepreneurial spirit, avoid demanding a type of support from politicians that is not the regular task of politics. The demand for guarantees is right at the top of the list. As entrepreneurs, we cannot complain about ever higher tax demands if, on the other hand, we demand more and more risk assumption by the state. The state can only spend what it first collects from taxpayers. And it can take on debt, which then has to be repaid by future generations. All of this has an impact on us and is largely determined by our social and entrepreneurial demands

In my view, it is a shared entrepreneurial responsibility to keep the state free of such demands. We have had the positive experience that simply focussing on networks and framework conditions opens far more doors than asking for subsidies, funding or guarantees.

In view of the role of investors, it is obvious that any risk minimisation is gladly accepted. However, the example of

Lilium and the failure of the massive public pressure for a state guarantee makes it clear that this approach is by no means a panacea for the company's continued existence, but rather represents a substantial risk. Not least because of the fundamental lack of legal entitlement to state guarantees.

Entrepreneurship offers the opportunity for prosperity, harbours the risk of failure and carries a shared responsibility for employees and partners in the value chain. The more seriously you take this responsibility, including the opportunities and risks, the more important the role of politics as a framework provider and networker becomes from your perspective.

How to read

»THE ROLE OF POLITICS«

› What legal framework conditions apply to my innovation?

› What improvements do I see in the legal framework?

› Am I already actively approaching politicians today to talk to them about improving the framework conditions?

› Do I only have my innovation or overarching advantages in mind when I make suggestions for improvement?

› How do I use the network of politicians today?

› How do I immunise myself against the all-too-easy demand that politicians bear my entrepreneurial risks and leave the profits to me?

› What contribution can I make as an entrepreneur to support the return of politics to its traditional area of application of setting the framework?

REAL NETWORKS AND GENUINE INTEREST

What's inside

Innovation thrives on the interest and support of many. On the way to realisation, the »community« of innovation continues to grow. The innovation develops its own appeal. People from other areas approach the innovator and offer their support. However, the interest is not always genuine. Then their own motives and optimisation goals take centre stage and the innovation becomes a means to an end. Nevertheless, it is good to be confronted with growing interest and increasing support. This episode looks at the particular importance of genuine networks and sincere interest.

The episode

Friendship is a true gift. A gift that is given from two sides. Not just once, but continuously. And we all know that you can count real friends on just one hand. Friends are genuinely interested in each other, they help each other through thick and thin. That's why real friendships are so valuable, so enduring, so powerful. Friends make you feel safe, even when things aren't going so well.

The same applies to genuine networks and sincere interest. Innovation becomes easier when you get help from outside. A genuine interest inspires one's own creative power. Real networks help each other without optimising themselves or holding out their hand for every favour. We have received these gifts along the way, and we consistently give back.

Over the years, our innovation has gone through some ups and downs with our inventor. Along with it, entrepreneurs have also suffered some heavy losses. When we dared to make a fresh start after a hostile takeover and forced separation from the previous team, we inevitably came to the point of looking for partners for subsequent series production. With open arms and genuine interest, we approached partners who had themselves been shipwrecked by the group responsible for the hostile takeover. We made no secret of our approach. We did not exaggerate our new development status. We simply asked, with an open mind, under what conditions it would be conceivable and attractive for these potential partners to join us in a new attempt to realise our innovation. And we were welcomed with open arms.

This enquiry was preceded by our actual restart. Building on the discovery of our HPB Solid-State Electrolyte, we were able to solve the last puzzles of the precursor technology and rethink series production. So, we had already made the decision to restart and implemented it organisationally. We had already done our homework. In the initial dialogue with our preferred partner for a significant part of the plant construction, the first step was to sound out our attitude to the negative experiences in the context of the predecessor technology. This was followed by a detailed discussion of the new answers to the unresolved issues at the time. The highlight, which still gives me goosebumps today, was the statement: »Let's put the past to one side and look forward to a successful future together.« This was not about exploiting an information gap to maximise one's own advantage. This was about nothing less than exploring an honest mutual interest and building a real network.

As a result, we put together a team that took care of answering all the detailed questions relevant to production with the considerable commitment of all those involved and by bringing in additional partners. This is particularly unusual because the familiar world of production construction ticks completely differently: There, it's all about a tender-led bidding process in which the client's specifications and requirements are translated into a bid. As a rule, the most favourable bidder is awarded the contract. Such an approach has some serious disadvantages for innovation development. On the one hand, the burden of defining the requirements lies solely with the innovator, while the ideas of the technology partners are held back due to the uncertain commissioning situation and competition with other providers. On the other hand, the cost-oriented selection of a realisation partner does not necessarily lead to the selection of the best partner. We know from established large

German industrial companies that there are departments accompanying such a bidding process that calculate the probability and scope of expected supplements based on incomplete specifications in order to guarantee the overall profitability of the project with the most favourable initial bid and lucrative supplements. Nobody benefits from this.

Instead, we have communicated from the outset that we work without competition in the individual partner positions. We live this commitment. And this commitment is reciprocated. When asked whether we might not fall into a cost trap as a result, we can only answer that the mentality of such cooperation is more about cost efficiency than one-sided sales optimisation. After all, the technology offers the potential for an attractive growth story. However, this requires a competitive offer. In this respect, each individual partner actively thinks about how risks can be minimised and costs reduced – without the worry of being outbid by someone else on price. This type of co-operation releases very special innovative forces. On a business level, it corresponds to the few genuine friendships that are worth investing in for all parties involved.

What it's all about

In an entrepreneurial context, real networks and sincere interest are comparable to the few genuine friendships that accompany and enrich our lives. Business friendships are not one-way streets either. They thrive on the fact that you can rely on each other and are there for each other – even when things get difficult.

This attitude is a rare case in today's reality. All too often, the focus is on self-optimisation at the expense of others. In the process, we lose sight of the fact that the optimisation of a group with mutual appreciation is more powerful than individual self-optimisation.

You can also find such partnerships for the realisation of your innovation. All you have to do is show a genuine interest in the expertise and sensitivities of your partners and be reliable partners yourself. Keep your word. Offer the kind of co-operation you would offer your friends. You will see that this attitude is already pleasantly unhinging the traditional rules of cooperation based on the exploitation of an information gap for self-optimisation. You will feel more comfortable working together. You will notice that your partners will start to think along with you in terms of realising your innovation.

What is interpreted as weakness or naivety by companies that are unable to deal with this will prove to be a solid foundation for the realisation of your innovation: real networks and genuine interest make the difference.

How to read

»REAL NETWORKS AND GENUINE INTEREST«

› What connects me to my real friends?

› Do I already have business partners who are friends to me on an entrepreneurial level?

› How do I find and make the right friends for the realisation of my innovation?

› Am I honestly interested in working together, as I expect my partner to be?

› Am I a rock for my partners – even if someone else is supposedly offering me the same service for much less?

› Do I help others as much as I accept help from others?

› How do I ensure in my area of responsibility that my network partners benefit properly from the network?

BOTTLENECK MANAGEMENT

What's inside

We are all familiar with bottlenecks. These are situations in which we feel or expect a shortage. Bottlenecks can take many different forms. The most obvious are bottlenecks associated with resources. However, there are also other bottlenecks that are more subtle, such as obstacles to concluding contracts. Bottlenecks are also sometimes highly variable over time. What was a bottleneck yesterday may not be one tomorrow and vice versa. This episode looks at the difference between a real bottleneck and a good excuse and how important it is to eliminate real bottlenecks.

The episode

As technology developers, we have to answer many technical questions. These include measurements, production processes and application issues. We need resources to answer such questions: people, machines and materials. If there is a shortage in one of these areas, we quickly speak internally of a »bottleneck«. We are then unable to answer basic questions because the prerequisites for doing so are lacking. Such a bottleneck can quickly turn into a mental block. The inevitable consequence is a standstill combined with a stalemate between eliminating the bottleneck and resolving it.

However, resolving the stalemate between eliminating bottlenecks and resolving standstills is only necessary if a bottleneck actually exists or threatens to arise. Until then, another task is critical to success: listening and thinking. After all, there are often many roads that lead to Rome. However, before alternative routes to Rome can be explored and finally taken, it is essential to understand the problem behind the supposed bottleneck in detail. This is precisely where many managers and innovators systematically get stuck. The detail is often annoying. It takes time. It requires concentration. It needs attention. It needs an alert mind. Otherwise you won't get to the real root of the problem.

It is astonishing how often bottlenecks arise simply because the meaning and purpose of the task are not understood at some point. Or that the nature and scope of the task simply seem impossible in view of the current resources available. Then, in no time at all, you find yourself in a bottleneck discussion, which is actually a sham discussion at its core. The bottlenecks are then supposed to lead to the realisation that this task or requirement should be put on the back burner. The »objective« impossibility should become the foundation of the consensus of rejection.

We had such a discussion at the beginning of the expansion of our own production facility. Our aim was to build a defined quantity of sample cells that would help us make significant progress in answering relevant questions for series production. The problem was that we needed these cells quickly. So we had a discussion about what exactly was missing in order to be able to produce the desired quantity of sample cells in the hoped-for short time. Of course we lacked machines and materials, and of course we had a professional discussion about alternatives. However, we only realised the actual bottleneck at the very end. When our head of technology development thought he was in an ultimate defence discussion because of our insistence, it burst out of him: »It won't do me any good if you provide me with the machines and materials on the ramp. If this is to succeed at all, then I need Klaus!« That was the bottleneck. After half a day of discussion. At the time, Klaus was an employee from our early days near Bonn. He worked at a chemical company that had once belonged to our inventor's friend. This friend made it possible for us to make a new start in his laboratory. It was in his laboratory that our inventor discovered our unique HPB Solid-State Electrolyte and built our first HPB Solid-State Batteries. Klaus had been supporting us for some time in this initial phase. But when we moved to our own production site, Klaus was no longer available to us simply because of the physical distance.

And this is exactly where what I call bottleneck management begins. Because now it was clear where the real bottleneck was. We needed Klaus. And we needed him yesterday rather than today. We declared the recruitment of Klaus a top priority without further ado. Of course, bottlenecks don't disappear just because they are declared a matter for the boss. This is more of a symbolic »upgrade« that says nothing more than giving the elimination of this bottleneck the highest priority. And, of course, luck is also part of it. Our luck was that the circumstances were favourable for us and for Klaus. We built the model in two stages. In stage 1, we made Klaus a lucrative offer for three weeks of support in our factory. He was able to realise this without falling into disrepute with his employer at the time. Once he was with us, we asked him for his »hygiene factors« at level 2. These are the conditions under which a decision can be made without any future regrets. Conditions that are sustainably favourable compared to the decision not to take action. No jockeying for the best possible conditions from the company's point of view. We wanted to win Klaus over at all costs. And that's exactly what we did.

Bottlenecks are characterised by the fact that there is no alternative to eliminating them. Until then, they are often good excuses. Addressing the reasons why certain things take longer than planned is just as important as consistently and continuously questioning the necessity behind the requirement. This is a real challenge, especially when different disciplines come together. Sales and manufacturing are such a pairing for us. The production facility is our guarantor for the preparation of series production. It is also the cradle of our scientific participation. This is what we call the need to publish our results in relevant scientific journals. Better visibility in the scientific world automatically leads to better visibility among analysts, media representatives and ultimately potential customers. Our sales department has the task of winning customers for our technology. However, different questions and requirements are always posed to test cells. There is soon talk of the need for technical due diligence. This, in turn, leads to the perception of the risk of an ongoing defocusing of manufacturing activities. This risk can best be averted with the help of a bottleneck discussion.

This is the part where we improve together and as a team every day. Eliminating perceived bottlenecks starts with questioning the real need. For example, we realise that the weaker their commitment and the further away they are from the topic, the more »evidence« and »visual material« prospective customers need for our technology. The requirements thus become a pawn between our sales department and our prospective customers, which we have played through for a long time directly in the production facility. We do this in the hope that this will enable us to take the decisive step in the customer relationship towards commitment.

We have now learnt that this is often not the result of our efforts. Too often, we have internalised external requirements. We are now taking a different approach: we have not only standardised the technical due diligence process and attached a price tag to all additional services, such as consulting and sampling. We have also started to scrutinise the requirements of our prospective customers to see if they are necessary – before we pass them on to our production facility as a requirement. It's amazing how many requirements simply dissolve when you talk about their sense and nonsense with the interested party, once you put a price tag on their fulfilment. In the end, it's also about the question: »What's in for us?« In the internal competition for resources, we have to reprioritise every day. And we would do well to prioritise priority 1 every day. Once Priority 1 has been completed, this does not mean that Priority 2 on the list will automatically become Priority 1. This is where we consciously interpose reprioritisation. In this way, we can ensure that we take care of the topics with priority 1 every day.

What it's all about

Bottlenecks appear in many different forms. What they have in common is that there is no alternative to resolving them in order to resolve the standstill they create. However, not every restriction has what it takes to become a bottleneck. Many situations perceived as bottlenecks dissolve when you question their necessity or relevance for achieving the goal or the next step. Then they suddenly appear milder, namely as a good excuse. The longer the perceived bottleneck withstands scrutiny, the better the excuse. The distinction between a bottleneck and an excuse is so important because a bottleneck is a threat, and an excuse throws sand in the gears. Both are bad. But both require a different solution strategy. It is of fundamental importance for this distinction to listen to everyone involved and to understand their point of view in detail. It is only on this basis that you are able to discuss possible alternatives. Changing the method is often enough to achieve the same goal by other means and thus outside the perceived bottleneck. Partnerships, for example, can work wonders. However, this is not possible if you don't listen and if you don't understand what the other person is actually trying to achieve behind the scenes.

Bottleneck management is therefore essentially a cognitive process that aims to utilise resources as efficiently as possible and focus on what is really missing. This is often less than you think, and it is often different than you assume. Bottleneck management of this kind is everyone's business. It is a skill that you can practise. Refrain from judging the other person's statements before you have understood their content in detail. Be aware when your statements are not understood and make sure that you are understood. Take off the blinkers of your own perspective and open yourself up to the idea that nobody gets up in the morning with the aim of making mistakes. So there must be something right about your counterpart's position. Check what alternatives would be conceivable to achieve the same goal – after you have jointly established that achieving this goal that you are discussing so intensively is really necessary for your innovation. Play bottleneck management like a nice-sounding instrument and don't use it like a calculator. Bottleneck management is first and foremost expectation management with and between people with their individual passion for your innovation.

How to read

»BOTTLENECK MANAGEMENT«

› How do I differentiate between bottlenecks and excuses today, and are both sufficiently transparent?

› How much do I dominate with my own opinion and don't listen properly?

› Am I being understood correctly today or do I need to improve here?

› Do we attach appropriate importance to bottle-neck management?

› Am I giving the real bottlenecks the necessary attention to eliminate them?

› Do I motivate or frustrate those around me when I talk about bottlenecks?

› How do I ensure that everyone is sufficiently aware of the importance of bottleneck management for efficiency and enjoyment with the innovation and in the company?

OPPORTUNITY OR RISK

What's inside

The realisation of an innovation is generally associated with enormous opportunities. But it is also associated with risks. The extreme is always involved: the risk of failure. The total loss. The decision to take the risk is made at the moment when the innovator sets out on the journey of realising their innovation. The official starting point of this journey is the founding of the company. The innovation has now reached the stage where the innovator is ready to implement it. Co-founders, family members and partners are invited to accompany this journey. This episode explores why the greatest risk has already been taken when a company is founded and why it is therefore particularly worthwhile to seize the opportunity from this point onwards.

The episode

There is no opportunity without risk. The elimination of risk turns opportunity into security. Innovation is first and foremost an opportunity. When a company is founded, the innovator believes that this opportunity is so great that it is worth embarking on the journey. A journey with many adventures and hardships. With joy and despair. With highs and lows. As in Tollkien's »Lord of the Rings«, the Innovator also benefits from gathering companions around him in order to achieve what he would not be able to do alone.

Everyone is motivated by the opportunity to innovate. Nobody knows the way, because it is an innovation because nobody has done it before. The excitement feels good and is fuelled by a never-ending stream of happiness. Over time, this initial euphoria gives way to reality. You realise that the path is anything but an easy walk. At the same time, you are fuelled by pride at the milestones you have reached. The value of the path you have already travelled becomes a driving force, a source of motivation for the next stage. This value becomes a value in itself. A value that increasingly becomes a value to be protected. Like the ring for Gollum.

From now on, every next step harbours the risk of losing what has already been achieved. Everything you have worked so hard for so far. Fear of loss takes the place of euphoria. The focus on risk gains the upper hand. For me, this is comparable to the career path of many adults. After school, the door to the world was open to all of us. In my generation at least, we were generally free to choose where we wanted to go professionally. We weighed up opportunities and decided on a direction. If we didn't like it, we made a new decision. Always in the knowledge that we could achieve anything we wanted. That was the time when we couldn't afford anything but still enjoyed life to the full. Once we had successfully started our careers, we were able to enjoy the sweet taste of our first earned money. Our standard of living rose and with it our supposed happiness. Those who could and wanted to, started a family, bought a house or found happiness in travelling around the world. And very gradually, this standard became a value in itself. Changing jobs increasingly became a risk. After all, you would have had to reassert yourself and might have lost your standard. I discussed this development up and down with my twin brother at the end of our thirties and the beginning of our forties. We finally came to the extremely moving question for both of us: when exactly do you stop dreaming? During this time, we both made the decision to completely reorient ourselves. To seize the opportunities of entrepreneurship for ourselves, to leave the supposedly safe harbour of salaried employment. Supported by our families, we were allowed to dream again.

Today, we work together and side by side on battery innovation. He with his partners and the joint engineering office, I as CEO of HPB, the technology developer of this innovation. We are both characterised by the fact that we have an unconditional will to implement and perceive a day without a focus on opportunities as a lost day. Both professionally and privately. For us, however, this does not mean that we turn a blind eye to existing risks. On the contrary!

A clear focus on the opportunities allows you to recognise the risks just as clearly. The art lies in dealing with the risks so that the opportunities can be realised. One of the biggest risks of a technology innovation is the leap into series production. This project can fail technically if you have not done your homework before investing in series production. But the project can also fail if no financing can be found. This is because the pressing question of when production will finally begin systematically ignores the fact that the necessary financial resources must be available for series production. I wrote the following message to a friend in response to his self-doubt due to his promise to set up production, the unexpected length of time it took to find investment capital and the increase in these nagging questions after the start of production: »Exactly! You've been promising it for years too. And for years your company has not received any support from the capital market. Show me a single top manager who can set up series production without any money at all. If there was one, you would have failed miserably and been a miserable failure.«

Any financing for the establishment of series production is associated with risks. This is particularly true for us. With our battery innovation, we find ourselves in an absolute shark tank. Huge players, enormously large markets, announcement management wherever you look, a wave of failures of major battery projects in Europe. And the dilemma that we simply can't get the investment we need to set up series production in Europe. We are therefore forced to open up to other regions of the world. Regions where there is a different attitude towards innovation and its financing. These include the USA, China and the Middle East. Yes, these regions have their own rules of the game, their own cultural characteristics. In the Middle East, for example, it is apparently customary for various people and institutions to be »involved« in raising capital. Of course, there are also charlatans among them. But they exist everywhere. What is striking, however, is that the »charlatan density« is weighted completely differently from region to region, depending on one's own origin and cultural categorisation.

In such a context, how do you get the opportunity without courting risk perception due to possible failure and not even pursuing this opportunity due to your preconceptions or abandoning it prematurely on the way to your goal? We have found a solution that invites you to rethink the way you deal with opportunities and risks for your own company. It is a model that is certainly unusual, and yet it works.

Together with one of our licensees, we decided to externalise the risk of the investment in the loan disbursement to risk partners in order to take advantage of an opportunity for a loan from the Middle East. In concrete terms, this means that the necessary payments were not made by the licensee, but by »external third parties« from the company's perspective. This reduced the risk for the licensee to zero. The chance of receiving the loan, and therefore the risk of possible fraud, did not change as a result. However, we have thus separated risk and opportunity. We used two levers to compensate for the risk assumption by our risk partners: On the one hand, we linked an attractive bonus payment to the disbursement of the loan, which was aligned with the risk loan. On the other hand, we compensated for the risk by transferring shares in the licence holder to our risk partners. This allowed us to give the risk partners a share in the actual opportunity of the company. Their advantage was therefore not exclusively linked to the potential fraud risk of such a loan. As a result, this model enabled us to offer a very favourable entry into the licensee and – without any financial burden for the company – we were given the opportunity to obtain a loan that would finally enable us to finance the first series production.

This example shows that it is not always a matter of weighing up opportunity against risk. It is sometimes advantageous to systematically separate opportunity and risk in order to preserve the opportunity and encapsulate the risks, making them bearable for all those involved should the risk actually materialise. As a result, we must not forget the spirit of the company's founding, which was to endeavour to build up production and achieve success. Without taking the risks outside Europe, the only option would be to face certain death in instalments within Europe.

What it's all about

The title of this episode plays with the obvious trade-off between opportunity and risk and a digital decision between the two. However, risk management is not about eliminating risks. Rather, it is about making the occurrence of risks bearable for all those involved. Only against the background of tolerable risks can the associated opportunities be pursued in a justifiable manner. There are therefore smarter design options than a digital weighing up of opportunity against risk. To achieve this, it is necessary to effectively encapsulate the risk so that it does not affect the spirit of the start-up, namely the successful realisation of the innovation. Conversely, it is necessary to grant an attractive share of the opportunity to those who help encapsulate the risk. This makes it possible to create a more favourable situation for all participants compared to their individual starting situation. This means that no-one is worse off if the risk materialises than if the alternative is not taken.

This model does not change the probability of occurrence

of the risk at all. This is because the risk of failure is generally not affected by it. However, it does allow us to fully focus on the opportunity. On the opportunity for a breakthrough in series production. If the risks materialise, i.e. the financing falls through for whatever reason, everyone around will stand up and bleat: »It was clear from the start. You should have seen that. What a management failure.« However, if you have balanced the model correctly, this accusation will not come from any member of the risk and profit distribution community. Their deal is still favourable. Then it's just a matter of focussing on the next opportunity. If the risks do not materialise, i.e. the financing is successful, everyone will say that they would have done exactly the same, that the model is absolutely obvious, a »no brainer«. This shows that the outsiders are always right. But it also shows that it is your responsibility to focus on the opportunities. Because if you focus on risk, you will miss the opportunities that will help you to fulfil the spirit of the start-up.

How to read

»OPPORTUNITY OR RISK«

› What is the focus of opportunities in my current everyday life?

› What do risks do to me and how do I deal with risks?

› What about my intercultural competence, my international communication skills?

› Am I weighing up opportunities against risks?

› What options do I see for structurally and systematically separating opportunities and risks?

› Am I prepared to give up a decent slice of the cake in return for external risk assumption?

› Who could I include in the circle of beneficiaries of such a model?

SKIN IN THE GAME

What's inside

When implementing innovations, inner drive, conviction and the necessary expertise are important drivers for success. However, these driving forces are difficult to measure. The exact implementation roadmap is too uncertain, the innovation environment too uncertain. This uncertainty is perceived and addressed differently by two relevant protagonists: The innovator would like to draw from the full and necessary resources and time, to lead his innovation to success without external pressure. Investors would like to receive maximum security for their financial risk assumption. It therefore appears to be advantageous from two perspectives if the innovator is fully committed to his innovation and thus has his »skin in the game«. This episode looks at what else is involved.

The episode

»Skin in the Game« is one of the investors' »eternal phrases«. It sounds particularly impressive when accompanied by a slight lisp. This phrase is flanked by a whole series of questions aimed at finding out how comprehensively the innovator identifies with his innovation and how much risk he has taken and is prepared to take in order to make the innovation a success. The evaluation of the answers given by the innovator is primarily concerned with forward-looking statements. From the investors' point of view, the past is often of secondary importance, as the past cannot be changed anyway and the need for capital does not come from the fact that the right course has already been successfully set in the past. Otherwise you wouldn't be sitting together.

Taken to a very simple level, many investors believe it is advantageous if the innovator has taken and continues to take so much risk that he literally loses everything in the event of failure. Then, according to the common hypothesis, the innovator will do everything in their power to make their innovation a success. Unconditionally. These investors like to call this »sufficient« »Skin in the Game«. But this hypothesis is not only wrong, it is also dangerous. Dangerous for the innovator, dangerous for the innovation and therefore also dangerous for the investor. This model is reminiscent of the gladiator fights in ancient Rome, which still take place underground today. There, gladiators fought for life and death. The audience could watch the spectacle unleashed. They didn't have to fear for their lives. For them, there was only the thrill of being a voyeur. The situation is similar for investors of this school of thought: of course, they don't put all their eggs in one basket either. In other words, they are by no means as attached to the success of the innovation as the innovator, who is prepared to lose everything.

Such investors ride in on too high of a horse. They are prepared to accept that their gladiator will die. Then they simply bet on a new gladiator next time. The main thing is not to lose the fun. And this is precisely the crux of this school of thought: only when the innovator and the investors share the same passion for innovation, inspire the innovator's inner drive, share the innovator's conviction and willingly contribute the missing, necessary expertise for implementation, do these important drivers for success work in the same direction. If these driving forces work against each other, they neutralise each other at best. In the worst case, they destroy each other and that is the end of innovation.

In the early phase of our company, we had the opportunity to speak to an investment committee. The main question that moved the gentlemen on this panel was whether we had already invested everything we could. Our answer was given carelessly and too quickly. It was: »No. Just like you, we can't afford to put all our eggs in one basket.« An annoying, serious and unnecessary mistake at the time. An answer in the heat of the moment. The cancellation came during the meeting. We didn't have enough »Skin in the Game«. It is pointless to argue about whether our company development would have taken a different course if we had simply said »yes«. However, it is certainly not pointless to think about whether such investors are the right partners for the realisation of the innovation.

At its core, the basic idea of »Skin in the Game« is based on systematic scarcity. A scarcity that ideally represents a permanent existential threat to the innovator. Only then – according to the hypothesis – will the innovator do their best to realise the innovation. However, fear is generally the worst counsellor. So why should this counsellor be permanently placed at the innovator's side? You can't work freely with your back against the wall. Only very few people can actually cope with such a burden. This also eliminates the need for necessary investments because you can't save up for them. This delays development and, at the end of the day, poses a substantial risk to the successful realisation of the innovation.

What it's all about

It's about correctly categorising the question about your »Skin in the game«. Which direction does this question come from? Is the idea of your existential fear as the strongest drive for success behind it? No matter what situation you find yourself in: Don't let anyone put fear at your side as a counsellor.

It is important and right that you devote yourselves wholeheartedly to your innovation. However, no one should expect you to jeopardise your entire existence for your innovation. It is much more important to have a clear idea of the next steps, the business model and the key requirements for the successful realisation of your innovation. Drawing from the full should not be equated with waste. It's about getting sufficient funds for the necessary investments – this explicitly includes overcoming your existential fears through adequate remuneration.

If your innovation and the associated opportunity is »only« a chance for the investor to increase his money without your drivers working in the same direction, you and your innovation will become a gladiator for the investor. You may be lucky and successfully realise your innovation. But with every step you take, you will feel the burden of existential fear from »Skin in the Game«. This is the greatest burden you can place on yourself and your environment. Therefore, check carefully which intention is connected to the question of your »Skin in the Game«. An invitation to a barbecue is only associated with the prospect of an enjoyable evening if you are not the meat on the grill.

How to read

»SKIN IN THE GAME«

› Does my potential investor share my passion for innovation?

› Do the ideas and approaches of the potential investor inspire my inner drive to realise the innovation?

› Does my potential investor share my convictions for the realisation of my innovation?

› Can the potential investor provide the expertise I lack and need for realisation?

› How important is my private well-being to my potential investor?

› What is my potential investor's »Skin in the Game« for me and my innovation?

› Does it feel good and right for me to work with this investor, or is my pleasure reduced to the short-term relief of financial support?

WHEN THE IDEA DIES

What's inside

We hear from almost every successful innovation that the road to success has been very tight at least once. The innovation, which is now so clear and shiny for all to see, narrowly escaped death. There are more examples of the death of an innovation than there are of the path to success. This is the hard fate of innovators and their innovations. This episode looks at the mechanisms that take effect when an idea dies and what can be done about it.

The episode

An innovation is a special creature. Due to the inventiveness of the innovator, it has its own soul and, in the form of a company, its own body. For me, the death of an idea is comparable to a person freezing to death. This death does not come suddenly, it comes gradually. The body defends itself. The body reacts. The body decides. Until it can no longer do so. Death comes at the end. On the way there, there are a number of measures that can help you escape death by freezing to death. Essentially, however, only one thing helps: warmth.

Before we venture to transfer freezing to the death of an idea, we should visualise the process of freezing using the human body as an example. From a medical point of view, this process is a three-stage process and is based on the fact that the human body is able to maintain a constant temperature despite varying external circumstances. If the external influences become too strong, the body takes measures that become increasingly radical in their consequences as the body temperature falls. Firstly, the body tries to produce the missing heat through muscle tremors. This muscle trembling occurs automatically when it gets too cold. At the same time, the blood vessels contract so that the extremities are supplied with less blood. This allows the body to concentrate heat on the inner core. The reduced circulation ensures that the cold blood remains in the outer regions and the warm blood in the core. If the body temperature continues to drop despite these countermeasures, consciousness gradually becomes clouded. It can go so far that the mind produces nonsense. Doctors refer to this condition as cold depression. At the same time, reflexes disappear and muscle tremors stop. If the body temperature drops even further, unconsciousness occurs, cardiac arrhythmia causes respiratory and circulatory arrest, which is signalled by an irregular and weak pulse. On the borderline to actual death, the body passes through the stage of apparent death, which is characterised by the fact that it is difficult to tell from the outside whether the person is still alive or already dead due to the low level of bodily functions.

As difficult as it is to imagine one's own death, it is helpful to transfer death by freezing to the death of an idea. This is because the main cause of death by freezing is an external cold effect that leads to an abnormally low body temperature. Only rarely is death by freezing an »internal matter«, a disruption of temperature regulation by the hypothalamus. Another good message in this comparison is that this death does not come suddenly, but announces itself and can be stopped and the damage minimised by the timely supply of warmth.

In terms of innovation, a company's body temperature is best described by its liquidity. The ability to pay bills and keep its own activities running. In the image of death by freezing, decreasing liquidity is comparable to a falling body temperature, and heat is comparable to the injection of capital into the liquidity reserve. The anatomical comparison also provides significant support: although the extremities are supplied with less blood when freezing to death, they are not shed as in a lizard, which can shed its tail when attacked by a predator, which then simply grows back. On the contrary, after overcoming hypothermia, all body parts should still be present and fully functional again. Amputations only have to be carried out in extreme emergencies. These are then carried out externally and therefore do not belong in the canon of the body's own protective measures.

This perspective is important, as when liquidity is declining, the first thing that is thought about too often is which »body parts« can be parted with. Suggestions such as making employees redundant, selling the »silverware« or even targeted insolvency to outsource personnel costs come to mind. These are all measures that rely on the »loss of body parts«. Measures that the freezing body does not have on its mind and that can only be implemented as an »*ultima ratio*«, as very last option, by an external surgeon. In this view, the perspective of the imminent death of the idea dominates the thoughts. The question of the consequences of this separation of body parts after defence against death by freezing does not even come to mind. To make this more tangible, the following consideration helps: Personnel costs are usually the main drivers of running costs. Therefore, making staff redundant often seems to be an obvious solution. However, this measure comes with the risk that the redundancies will cause such uncertainty and excessive demands on the people directly and indirectly affected that they will have lost their confidence in the common path after the cold spell has passed, i.e. after the influx of fresh liquidity, and will no longer be available to implement the innovation. Skills shortages primarily affect those companies for which employees are an interchangeable resource that should be purchased as cheaply as possible.

Equally short-sighted are measures that focus on »selling the silverware«. Once the silverware has been sold, the source of this solution strategy dries up. If it is not ensured at the same time that the cause of the cold effect from outside is overcome, this measure is as warming and helpful as a flash in the pan. Such measures lack sustainability in terms of the survival of the innovation once the cold has been overcome.

So, before measures are taken to reduce liquidity requirements within the company, for example by letting employees go, or to increase liquidity in the short term, as is possible on a one-off basis through the sale of silverware, the key question is how new liquidity can be injected into the company from outside. What measures can I take to create the necessary trust in the right people so that they will support the company with fresh liquidity? How do I find these people and what do I offer them?

In essence, it is about »reinventing ourselves on the outside« instead of »short-term rescue on the inside«. This external reinvention takes time. After all, on the basis of sound financial planning, you have the best idea of when you will need fresh liquidity. The most important message in this context is: start this reinvention in good time. Get in touch with your environment and clarify what makes your innovation exciting for investors. Also think about what you have to offer if someone provides you with the liquidity you need. Stay flexible in your mind and focussed on the success of your project. Turn your gaze away from the threat of death by cold, as this will lead you into decisions that are detrimental to the continuation of your path after overcoming the liquidity bottleneck. In short: avoid the cold defence. Make a strict distinction between a flash in the pan and switching off the source of the cold. Concentrate your energies on the opportunities, because this is the only way to focus on your survival.

What it's all about

Hope is not a strategy. That is old management wisdom. However, hopelessness quickly leads in the wrong direction. In the image of cold death, it is the harbinger of cold depression. A disturbance of consciousness that focuses attention on the threat of death and the mitigation of its consequences. Measures such as going bankrupt, laying off employees and selling off the silverware all fall into this category. They lead to a creeping overstretching of the company and the people involved. Despair grows and the company finds itself surrounded by opponents of its own innovation, by enemies.

However, comparing the death of an idea to freezing to death has some very positive messages for you and your innovation: Essentially, it's about securing your liquidity. This only comes sustainably from the outside. Not from within by cutting back or separating company resources. If you can rule out an internal malfunction of your innovation hypothalamus, i.e. your innovation has a solid foundation in terms of content, you should focus on your environment. It's about your continuous »reinvention on the outside«, the perception of your innovation by those who can support you with fresh liquidity.

This makes your own roadmap all the more important. What is the next step needed to realise your innovation? This is much more important than an external target in the form of a condition for securing liquidity. Such conditions can lead to the level of ambition rising too high, which means that resources have to be increased, which in turn means that you will need more liquidity to survive in a shorter period of time. Focus on your plan. Win over supporters for it. Tell your story and offer a decent share of the opportunity to those who help you in this situation.

We consistently focus and combine opportunities for our innovation and our supporters. Our business model as a technology developer is based on the collection of licence fees. This keeps our cost structure relatively low in the long term. Nevertheless, we also have to keep an eye on liquidity and bridge the time until our licensees start production in such a way that we don't freeze to death on the way. In this way, we have already received various offers that were regularly accompanied by a very high price. Risks in the package leaflet that we would not be prepared to take without the pressure. With our consistent focus on realisation and opportunities, we always manage to reinvent ourselves on the outside. This consistency also helps us not to seize such supposed opportunities with package inserts, but to continue looking for the right supporters. Measures that structurally increase the need for liquidity may be a source of heat in the short term, but may lead to increasingly severe cold spells for the survival of your innovation much sooner and much faster.

Just as a body concentrates on its core functions without shedding body parts in the fight against the cold, you should see your people and resources for the realisation of your innovation as a core that must be protected at all costs. It is and remains the people who make the difference for your innovation – one way or another.

How to read

»WHEN THE IDEA DIES«

› Do I have a financial plan that gives me sufficient transparency about my company's liquidity?

› Am I paying the necessary attention to securing liquidity?

› Have I sensitised and activated all relevant people in my company for liquidity protection?

› Am I focussing on the opportunities or the risks of securing liquidity?

› How do I ensure that the solutions for securing liquidity are not a gateway to further, faster and more severe cold snaps?

› What measures can I take to create the necessary trust with the right people so that they support me with fresh liquidity?

› How do I find these people and what do I offer them?

CREATIVITY AS THE BEST RESPONSE TO RESISTANCE

What's inside

Resistance is the bulwark of the present. It is testimony to an excessive demand, testimony to a collective will for a certain »*status quo*«. Innovations are particularly affected by this. People want and need to be involved in change. Not all resistance to innovation is therefore insurmountable. Going "headfirst through the wall" is not always the easiest way. Nor does it guarantee success. Thinking up alternatives, rethinking in good time, generally remaining flexible for the path with a clear goal – this is the creativity that is needed to lead an innovation to success. Why resistance is even an indicator of innovative strength is the subject of this episode.

The episode

Yes, but…! Innovators often hear that. That's understandable. After all, it's about innovation, i.e. something new. However, »Yes, but...« also gets annoying over time. It chafes. Again and again, explanations are needed, again and again you feel like you're starting from scratch. The value of the innovation simply won't be recognised. However, »Yes, but...« also offers the opportunity to consistently scrutinise your own story. To examine whether what you share about innovation perhaps even necessarily causes uncertainty and doubt among those you want to convince and who are not yet »in the subject«. »Yes, but...« is the most harmless form of resistance. Its solution lies largely within the innovator's own area of responsibility.

Another stage is »friendly fire« from the immediate environment of the innovation and the innovator. In the broadest sense, this relates to disagreement about parts of the path to success or even diametrically opposed ideas about the right direction. This resistance costs a lot of energy, especially in internal relationships. However, it is no less important to overcome this form of resistance. The best way to do this is through communication, explanation and consensus. To achieve this, it is important to listen seriously to the respective points of view and to examine what potential for improvement they harbour. It is often the compromise between different perspectives that paves the way to success and makes it easier. Diametric opposites are problematic in this category of resistance. They can, for example, affect the fundamental orientation of the business model. We repeatedly encounter such a contradiction in the discussion about licensing our technology as opposed to setting up our own production. When all the substantive arguments have been exchanged, all the potential for improvement has been realised through consensus and pooling of the best ideas, and there is still disagreement about the best way forward, then a decision needs to be made. This decision can be conclusively justified after such a mature discussion and consideration and provides a reliable framework for further development. Looking back, it does not necessarily have to be the right path. However, the vying for the best path also wastes a lot of resources and, above all, does not provide any reliable orientation. If the decision is well-founded, resistance is rightly futile. This does not eliminate resistance, but categorises it. Incidentally, it does not mean that the substantive reasons for the resistance may not materialise further down the line. Then it is time to pause and question your own path again. However, a clear basis for decision-making is important for your own orientation and that of your companions.

An example from our business model illustrates this. Not everyone understands the business model of licensing. It sometimes seems much easier to think of technology development, production and market development from a single source. Building a group instead of an ecosystem of strong independent partners. In this discourse, all possible fields of application have been constructed in which the licensing business model would simply make no sense, particularly due to the premise of exclusivity, which makes sense for various reasons, such as only granting exclusive home storage in Germany to a single licence holder. The example where the exclusivity premise was rightly questioned was the automotive industry. Here, it is understandably impossible to allocate fields of application geographically and without overlaps. Nor do we want to develop batteries for the automotive industry. Accordingly, we have improved our business model here by licensing our HPB Solid-State Electrolyte to the automotive industry as a component for their battery development on a non-exclusive basis. »Yes, but...« and »Friendly Fire« have brought us an important step forward here. At the same time, we have clearly stuck to our business model of licensing because, despite intensive discussions, there are no convincing reasons in favour of the group model. Since then, a sensible compromise and a clear decision have provided the necessary security for the next steps.

Another relevant category of resistance is disappointment. This category is so treacherous for an innovation because it is based on unfulfilled promises. These can have a variety of causes. What they have in common, however, is that they can erode confidence in your own path, that they wear you down, that they cost you strength. Disappointments build up an inner resistance that grows as the extent of the disappointment increases. It is important to recognise the end of a disappointment as an opportunity to reinvent yourself. This is easier said than done. Nevertheless, it is good to realise this. The clearer the reasons for the disappointment are on the table and the more transparent you are about avoiding these reasons in the future, the more successful your own reinvention will be. Keeping a disappointment quiet, which often seems easier, narrows your view of opportunities and, in case of doubt, prevents you from using disappointments to strengthen yourself.

External resistance is particularly challenging. This includes over-critical reporting as well as the networks of the »*status quo*«. This resistance is sometimes so great that even seemingly easily available instruments, such as public funding, become unattainable. There is also a tendency in the European media landscape to write against innovation, rather than holding the reins for it. All of this is always done with the justification of »critical journalism« and the unassailability of »press freedom« in mind. The NZZ offers a particularly bad example of this under the headline »The 400 per cent fairy tale«: Here, a return on investment on an infrastructure investment in industrial storage with a term of 15 years is »confused« with an annual return on shares. In line with this serious error – intent would be even worse and can at least not be ruled out given the tendency of the article – the statement is categorised as a dubious stock market letter. And this from the pen of a journalist who calls himself a business journalist. This type of reporting is particularly prevalent in Europe. Lurid and negative news obviously sells better than positive news. The creative approach to dealing with this kind of total journalistic failure is to think back to our own childhood: we were regularly read fairy tales by our grandma and the good always prevailed in the end.

What it's all about

Resistance takes many forms. They occur inside and outside the innovation circle and are usually a sign that those who resist are overburdened. It is good to deal with resistance in a positive way. Not all resistance is unfounded. Rather, the confrontation offers the opportunity to question and optimise one's own procedural model, one's own path, one's own premises. Even a fundamental change of direction can help you on the way to the success of your innovation if it is well and conclusively justified.

However, there is also resistance that cannot be used to improve one's own path, even if it is read positively. Then you need a clear edge, a clear decision, a demarcation. Resistance that attacks the core of your innovation because it is intended to preserve or protect something else is particularly robust. For example, an outdated technological »*status quo*«.

I now believe that resistance is an indicator of the innovative strength of your innovation. The more your innovation challenges, the greater the change associated with it, the greater the resistance. Because innovation is usually at a resource disadvantage compared to the established world until it has established itself, it is all about your creativity in dealing with this resistance. Be prepared to reinvent yourself every day. Question the actual motives behind the resistance – not just the way it is presented. Carefully examine what improvements can be made for you and your innovation by actively and positively dealing with resistance. But also be clear about your boundaries. This strengthens your authenticity and ultimately increases the unagitated radiance of your innovation.

How to read

»CREATIVITY AS THE BEST RESPONSE TO RESISTANCE«

› What resistance am I currently facing?

› What is my previous reaction pattern to resistance?

› Have I made sure so far that I use resistance to strengthen myself?

› How can I improve my attitude and that of my organisation to dealing with resistance?

› Do I have a sufficiently broad repertoire of reactions?

› How can I improve my internal and external communication?

› Am I working with the right professionals to overcome resistance smartly?

DON'T LOSE FAITH

What's inside

The business of innovation is a daring endeavour. You have to have a fair amount of idealism to hold on to the idea that you can successfully realise an innovation in the face of adversity and resistance in Germany and Europe. For most people, embarking on this rocky road seems like a kind of self-abandonment. However, everything that we like to rest on in our affluent society only exists because people have believed in something and have remained true to their idea, vision and ultimately themselves. Faith moves mountains. This episode is about the fact that this is by no means a nonsensical saying.

The episode

Believing in something is no substitute for knowledge. But knowledge alone does not move mountains either. It takes motivation, a deep-seated inner conviction that the efforts involved in realising an innovation are worthwhile. There is an important basic rule for any small talk: avoid the topics of religion, politics and ideology. However, small talk is of negligible relevance in the context of innovation. Its penetration depth is too low when it comes to getting someone excited about something new. Deep-seated inner convictions are based on a foundation that can only be aptly described by the term »belief«. But what is this belief about in a world that is primarily concerned with measurability? Faith eludes all measurability. Nevertheless, it is precisely this faith that makes the decisive difference.

A striking example is all the winners of casting shows. If they hadn't believed in themselves, if they hadn't trusted that they had a special talent and if they hadn't dared to go on stage with this talent and face the jury and the audience, they wouldn't have won this format. But they did.

Implementing innovations is far more complex than taking part in a casting show. Nevertheless, it is valuable to illuminate the common core and talk about this elementary basis of success far away from any small talk: The belief in one's own success and the associated radiance. It's about any kind of belief that helps the innovator to stick to their idea, find the right supporters and, at the end of the day, make a contribution to social development with a successful innovation. It's about not selling your soul, realising that there is support and stability along the way and not losing confidence that the light at the end of the tunnel is not a locomotive, but the breakthrough of innovation into success.

Before I started implementing our battery innovation, I was on the verge of becoming a chronic pain patient thanks to a severe slipped disc. I regularly had to take heavy medication to make the day bearable and maintain my productivity despite the pain. I was at a point where I didn't even realise that I was falling into these pain phases more and more frequently. One day, I visited my oldest and best friend from university. We met when we enrolled at university. Since then, we have not only been linked by our consecutive matriculation numbers, but also by a deep friendship. During this visit, he suddenly said that he thought our friendship was stable enough to be damaged by what he would like to tell me. My interest was piqued and I was open to the person he wanted me to meet. A person with extraordinary abilities.

We quickly decided to visit her and she showed me in a session how she works. At the time, I had two fundamental concerns: I had swapped a well-paid job in a large company for self-employment so that I could devote myself fully to implementing innovations. This was supported at all times by my wife and my family. My first concern, which I had never discussed with anyone before, was that I was overburdening my wife with my drive for self-employment and entrepreneurship, thereby jeopardising our family and our personal happiness. My second, equally deep-seated concern was that I wasn't sure whether I was the right person to realise our inventor's innovation. Under no circumstances did I want my fascination with his invention, as possibly the wrong person, to inadvertently prevent the realisation of his life's work. I wanted to be sure that the right person would lead this idea to success. My first concern was unjustified, but my second concern was my problem. I had taken on too much of the burden of being solely responsible for the success of this battery innovation. A burden that we symbolically packed into a backpack and took off my shoulders. In addition to the increased confidence in my own actions, this was the last day that I had chronic back pain – until today. Since then, we have been working intensively together to realise the innovation. This has taught me a lot, including how to read my body's signals. For example, I can physically feel when someone is literally »stabbing me in the back«.

This meeting was like a turning point for me. I have always been open to the idea that there is much more out there than our mundane existence. Today I know that there are different levels of existence and that there are special people who can make contact with these levels. We call this access our »online service«. What I can give is my basic trust in this connection and my unshakeable belief that we are doing the right thing. Our path is anything but easy or simple. But it is a very good feeling to be supported – on all levels that are necessary for innovation.

What it's all about

The most important foundation of any innovation is the unshakeable belief of the innovator in their own idea. This belief helps to literally move mountains. And the path of an innovation to success could not be better described than by the task of moving mountains. Without this belief, there is a lack of confidence and self-assurance in one's own abilities. The foundation for one's own success is missing.

Even if we have found a very special approach for our path

with the »online service«, this does not mean that this is the way for every innovation, let alone for every innovator. Rather, it is about focussing on what will secure this critical ingredient for success, namely belief in innovation, in the long term. Every innovator has their own approach to this. Just as there are no blueprints for innovation, there are no blueprints for accessing this foundation.

You know the feeling when things feel really good. They give you strength and energy. They inspire and clear the way for the next stage. You also know the feeling when things don't feel good. They sap strength and cost energy. They drag you down and make it infinitely difficult to move on to the next stage. Perhaps it is this intuition, this simple compass, that is enough to make you realise that maintaining your belief in your own innovation and the benefits of your own commitment to its implementation is the most important prerequisite for your own success.

This faith is like an inner treasure. Do not allow this treasure to be damaged from the outside. Be open to all ways that strengthen you and your faith in innovation. It is not about closing your eyes to reality. Rather, it is about recognising different paths in the jungle of reality that can lead you towards success. As innovators, all eyes are on you. You must instil confidence in your companions that all efforts will indeed be worthwhile. It is up to you to be flexible with the challenges to your innovation, to regularly question whether the steps you are taking, the people you are surrounding yourself with, are suitable to achieve the goal. To do this, it is important to be able to pause. To seek the silence that you need to be able to think clearly and feel your own intuition. To seek the exchange that offers you the necessary perspectives.

I was amazed at how many people confirm the existence of an »online service« and agree with me that this connection provides a special grounding for the realisation of an innovation. Basic trust instead of doubt, acceptance instead of control, confidence instead of despair – these are the components that help you not to lose faith in yourself and your innovation.

How to read

»DON'T LOSE FAITH«

› Do I believe in my innovation and in my ability to lead it to success?

› Which people or skills am I missing?

› How unshakeable is my belief in my innovation as the foundation for success?

› Do I know how I can strengthen my belief in my innovation and where I might be blocking myself?

› Am I clear enough today to concentrate on the people and topics that give me strength and energy?

› What prevents me from letting go of people and issues that shake my faith in innovation and my confidence in the path, that cost me strength and energy?

› Do I know the sources from which I can refresh my faith in my innovation and my abilities and keep them alive, and am I already utilising these sources to a sufficient extent?

FRIENDSHIP ENDS WITH MONEY

What's inside

30 July is the International Day of Friendship. 04 December is International Bankers Day. As far apart as these two days are in the annual calendar, money and friendship literally do not go together. A reference to this experience can already be found in Shakespeare. Borrowing money from friends or family is often perceived as more problematic than lending money to friends or family. Fear, shame or a guilty conscience are the most common reasons for this. This episode looks at other perspectives on this saying with regard to innovation.

The episode

Friendship is a valuable asset. Here you feel safe, supported and carried. Friends share a strong bond. Sometimes you know the other person better than you know yourself. It is therefore all the more astonishing that for many, friendship actually ends when it comes to money. If you look at the origin of this saying, you realise that it usually refers to an emergency situation in which one person has to borrow money from another. Emotional closeness is seen as the main cause of possible quarrels. It is even suggested that the lender has to deal with the possibility of never seeing the loaned money again.

If you change your perspective, innovation offers the opportunity to become fabulously rich. This requires appropriate investment and risk-taking at the beginning. Wouldn't you want your friends and family to have a slice of this cake? What exactly is stopping so many people from thinking this way? Investors structurally assume risks that can lead to a total loss if they materialise. Incidentally, this risk also exists when buying shares on the stock market. Nobody is immune to the fact that risks, which are always associated with opportunities, can materialise. Transferred to the case of money lending, the risk-free case would be giving money away. Then you don't have to worry about whether you will see your money again. However, if you give money as a gift – for example, by giving generously to your family and friends in the event of success – you will, with a few exceptions, slide into a considerable gift tax burden beyond a tax-free amount.

However, there is also a completely different perspective that invites us to fundamentally rethink this principle of »friendship ends with money« in the context of innovation.

The traditional reluctance to approach friends and family is nothing other than paternalism. Patronising because the decision not to invest is made by the innovator's reluctance. Some friends and family members would certainly like to be perceived as responsible decision-makers when it comes to their own investment decisions.

This draws attention to a completely different aspect of an investment in innovation: trust and transparency. These are natural components of any friendship. And they should be the natural components of any investment in innovation. You should not – as is often required of investors in the due diligence process – have to literally take off all your clothes before being told whether and under what conditions an investment in the innovation is even conceivable. When initiating a relationship, you don't ask your potential partner for a full inspection in a restaurant on the first date. It's more about the sincerity that you cultivate with friends anyway. Honesty in relation to the opportunities and risks of innovation. The risks in particular are much more relaxed to talk about with friends, precisely because you know each other so well.

Friendship requires courage. You have to get involved with the other person. So that, in case of doubt, the other person knows you better than you know yourself. Only then can you let yourself go in a friendship. Courage also means letting the other person make their own decision about participating in the innovation, allowing them to make this decision in all friendship. Then there is no shame, no exploitation, no envy. Then it's not about wealth or power. Then it is only about the chance to get a piece of the cake if you are successful. It's about individual happiness. According to Aristotle, there are three types of friendship: friendship of pleasure, friendship of purpose and true friendship. All of these friends deserve to be allowed to make their own decisions about their investment in your innovation.

We were lucky enough to be able to win friends for our innovation several times who supported us financially. They did this fully aware of the risk of a total loss and with the unconditional consistency that only friends are capable of. Each time, we discussed both the opportunity and the risks at each stage of development transparently with each other. We also clearly agreed at all times that it was the sole decision of our friends to invest or not to invest, and we made sure that there was a fair balance between opportunity and risk. Thanks to this transparency and consistency, we have also been able to navigate the valleys together that would have been too deep for us without the support. We received support when »normal« investors were no longer »betting« on us. Yes, that is a moment of shame. But it is also a moment of immense gratitude. Gratitude for the friendship and gratitude for the help.

What it's all about

A kilo of friendship, please? No, you can't buy friends. We learn that as children. And that's a good thing. But does friendship stop at money? At least that's what we learnt as children. We don't talk about money. But when it comes to innovation, participation in innovation offers enormous opportunities in the event of success. And should we not let our friends share in these opportunities? We should leave this decision to our friends and family. If we take this decision away from them, we are patronising them and not taking them seriously.

It is important that you do not tie the offer to participate in your innovation to any expectations, either in favour of or against participation. You should also inform your friends and family just as transparently about the potential risks as any other investor. You will realise how clear and simple such discussions are if you dare to have them.

In situations where everyone else who is not so close to you is just keeping their fingers crossed for you without providing any financial support, you will find that friends and family who decide for themselves in favour of the opportunities and risks of your innovation will, when push comes to shove, be even more willing to help you get through critical situations. Friendship requires courage: courage to open up, courage to get involved, courage to trust, courage to allow yourself to be helped, courage to face honest criticism, courage to expect and accept the other person's decision. Courage is rewarded, says another saying. A saying that is as much a part of innovation as International Friendship Day and International Banking Day are in the same year.

How to read

»FRIENDSHIP ENDS WITH MONEY«

› Do I already have friends or family on board as supporters for my innovation?

› What are my reasons for not asking this group?

› How do I handle it when friends and family ask me if they can invest with me?

› What fears block me from approaching friends?

› How can I ensure a fair risk/reward balance?

› What helps me to realise that friends and family in particular can help me to overcome great difficulties?

› How brave am I as a friend – on each side of the friendship?

BETWEEN SEED AND GROWTH: THE DEATH VALLEY OF INNOVATION

What's inside:

Innovation has a hard time by nature. This is because it thinks differently and solves something differently than it has been done before. Technical innovations in particular fall into this pattern. At the time of its inventor, Rudolf Diesel, no more people wanted to see the diesel engine in the world than people want to think it out of the world today. Apps that dominate or even dominate our everyday lives today did not exist before the introduction of the iPhone. Here, too, resistance initially dominated. Innovations that rely on series production are characterised by a phenomenon that is far less relevant to software-based innovations or services: the importance of initial series production. This episode looks at the pitfalls that this entails for innovation.

The episode

An innovation is formally considered an innovation when it has successfully arrived on the market and become established. This term is therefore used to honour successful changes that make things possible in a different or completely new way and therefore represent a leap in development compared to the »*status quo*«. Like all changes, such changes are always associated with risks along the way and with their success. Avoiding change is also associated with risks. It is not without reason that this statement has a true core: If you don't keep up, you'll get left behind.

Accepting and overcoming many of the risks of change is easier with sufficient liquidity – as is sitting out change. However, it is precisely this liquidity that is often the critical point, the bottleneck of an innovation on its path to success. Surprisingly, it doesn't matter whether the innovation comes from an established company or a start-up. In established companies, the antagonist of liquidity is called »day-to-day business« or »cash cow«. Before innovations have the potential to overtake the »cash cows« of the present for the future, the focus on day-to-day business often dries up the liquidity for innovations. »Corporate innovation« therefore has its own internal challenges to overcome. This is why many large companies have launched accelerator programmes designed to bridge the gap between external speed and flexibility and a financially strong corporate structure. Start-ups are closely linked to the respective companies via such programmes and provided with the necessary funds in the initial phase. However, this connection in no way ensures that the innovation will be successful in such a »safe« harbour. Especially not if the innovation is later to be incorporated into the core business of the large company. Then the same mechanisms often take effect as with an innovation »from within«: day-to-day business, i.e. the present, trumps the future.

In the case of innovations outside established companies, liquidity often requires external financing, i.e. from investors, banks and subsidies. There are two basic phases, each of which follows its own structural rules: The early stage (seed) and the growth stage (growth) of an innovation. In the early stage of innovation, the realisation risks are still comparatively high. There are risks in three categories: Technology risks, production risks and market risks. The further an innovation progresses, the lower the risks in these three categories become. The company value increases accordingly. However, investors who specialise in the early stage of innovations are attracted by the leverage of investing as early as possible. In other words, at a time when the risk is still high and the company value – and therefore the exchange rate in company shares – is still low. The lower the risk, the lower the interest of this group of investors. There is an uncomfortable truth in this realisation: for the same target share in the company, investors have to put more and more money on the table over time. From this perspective, it is advantageous to invest in this innovation as early as possible. This is the only way to achieve the greatest possible diversification and thus spread risk while maximising opportunities with the limited funds available to investors. With this model, it is enough if a few innovations manage to »bite through« to success. For most investors of this type, it is also true that they can hardly afford a later entry themselves. Their pockets are often not deep enough for an innovation with production requirements to finance the first series production. As a result, they cannot afford series production at all. The other group of investors is the growth financiers. They shy away from risk. They are very well capitalised and can also easily finance infrastructure projects. This group has specialised in the growth stage of innovations. In this phase, the technology, production and market risks are generally overcome. It is »only« a matter of scaling the innovation. As a result, they only appear from the second series production line onwards.

There is a huge gap between these two groups, the early-stage investors (seed) and the growth financiers (growth). There are almost no areas of overlap. Even public organisations that are committed to promoting innovations of social importance have no solution to this problem. One example of such a public organisation is the »Bundesagentur für Sprunginnovationen«, i.e. the Federal Agency for Leap Innovations in Germany, SPRIND. For me, this gap, i.e. the achievement of the first series production, is best described as the »death zone of innovation« or the »death valley of innovation«.

From the perspective of many consultants and early-stage investors, the only solution to overcoming this death zone that is often propagated is: sell your innovation to a large company. The suspenseful thing about this advice is that the current »usual suspects« that guarantee success did not even exist 30 years ago. So these guarantors once set out on their own path and led their innovation to success. In doing so, they often crossed this death zone themselves and found creative solutions to survive. Solutions that seem obvious in hindsight and yet seemed impossible beforehand.

What it's all about

For innovations that require series production, the highest risk lies in the first series production line. Until then, there is no proof of producibility; until then, production and market risks cannot be reduced to zero. Your endeavour is therefore subject to a disproportionately high external risk assessment until then. Accordingly, reaching series production maturity is important for the breakthrough of your innovation.

You cannot start early enough to prepare for this death zone. This involves identifying suitable partners who can effectively help you to achieve your first series production, also in terms of external perception. You have a lot to give in return. Genuine co-operations are a particularly effective means. In these, it is advantageous for everyone involved to contribute their strengths to the success of the innovation. This requires the formation of a risk and profit sharing community. Neither the focus on risk sharing nor on profit sharing builds a stable co-operation. If the risk taker does not share in the profit, risk assumption is much less attractive for him. If the demand for profit sharing is outside the scope of those who bear the risk, the inclusion of such a partner in the profit pool is also less attractive. It is therefore a question of a balanced relationship between risk and profit sharing.

Appropriate caution is therefore required when selecting financing instruments. If the required company shares or interest rates are too high, this could jeopardise the implementation of the innovation due to changes in the decision-making process. To stay with the image of the »Death Valley of Innovation« that you usually have to pass through for your innovation on the way to the first series production, it is a matter of selecting the companions with whom you can master the challenges of the death zone. Cannibalism due to an imbalance in the incentive systems in the collaboration jeopardises the cohesion of the group and reduces your chances of reaching series production. For your innovation, selling your innovation to a large company also means joining a group to cross the death zone and not a well-air-conditioned party bus with sufficiently cool drinks.

How to read

»BETWEEN SEED AND GROWTH: THE DEATH VALLEY OF INNOVATION«

› Do I have a sufficient overview of the first series production?

› Do I know who I need to achieve series production readiness?

› Is my cooperation model sufficiently attractive and stable?

› Are there imbalances in the incentives for co-operation that could jeopardise cohesion along the way?

› How does my financing fit in with the distance still to be travelled until series production?

› Which people could help me through the death zone of innovation?

› How can I make the journey more attractive and therefore more promising for all companions?

THE PSYCHOLOGY OF INNOVATION – FROM THE IDEA TO THE MARKET

What's inside

The idea for an innovation is a significant moment. It is the incredible feeling of having been given something very special. An idea that substantially improves something that already exists or makes something possible that was previously impossible. At this moment, everything seems very clear. The steps are clear, the paths are short, and the resources required are manageable. But in many cases, this idea is the start of a long and arduous journey. A journey that sometimes demands everything from the innovator, brings them to the brink of suffering and often challenges them beyond the limits of their own motivation and enthusiasm. A journey that all too often leads to situations where you would rather turn back or even stop. This episode is about how wonderful the journey is despite all the hardships.

The episode

Reading stories about successful innovations and their innovators is like travelling back in time. What an overwhelming moment it must have been for Christiaan Barnard in Cape Town in 1967 when his patient Louis Washkansky woke up with a new heart. This was preceded by a moment of relief the day before, at 05:52 a.m. on Sunday 3 December 1967: the freshly transplanted heart was beating again. These are moments for eternity. Moments that belong to very special people. People who have given everything for their innovation. People who have sacrificed themselves. Today, a heart transplant is a routine operation. The actual pioneering achievement is often forgotten. The innovation is taken for granted without ever having been there at any point on the way to the breakthrough.

What all innovators have in common is that they have a vision of something, can see something in their mind's eye that no one else has thought of before. For them, their idea is tangible, perceptible, touchable, feasible. The only challenge: this idea simply has to be realised. And this is exactly where the innovator's journey begins with their innovation in their luggage. A large portion of anticipation and hopefully enough naivety in the awareness of the upcoming experiences are part of the journey.

If you compare different successful innovations and their innovators, you realise that, as a rule, no innovator has led their innovation to success on their own. It is therefore first and foremost a question of finding the right companions. They bring with them qualities that the innovator lacks or that expand and complement their skills. It is in the nature of things that companions may only be able to accompany the innovator part of the way or may want new companions to join them. What is always important is the inner conviction and identification with the innovation, the purpose. Companions are never primarily interested in money, fame and recognition. They put themselves at the service of the innovation and the innovator and contribute their skills to its success. In this way, they become companions and differ significantly from the numerous free riders who become conspicuous primarily through self-optimisation along the entire path.

However, companions are only one part of an innovation's journey to success. The resources required to realise this innovation are also essential. This often involves far more than just financial resources. It is about access to knowledge, technologies and materials and, last but not least, the right business model. Here too, the main motivation for others to provide these resources lies in the appeal of the innovation and the innovator.

In order to attract and retain the right companions and necessary resources, it is crucial to represent your own innovation and the associated vision at all times and at every opportunity in such a way that the invitation to participate is gladly accepted. Once success has been achieved, it is in the nature of things that many fathers of success suddenly want to assert their claims. Free riders and those who want to bask in the glamour of innovation come crawling out of all the holes. The situation along the journey is completely different. Often enough, there is a lonely and fine line to tread, for example between delaying insolvency and survival. And all those who consistently keep their fingers crossed without making a contribution of their own only cost time in case of doubt and do not advance innovation and innovators.

It is helpful to realise that there is no blueprint for innovation. Every idea, every vision has its own laws and requirements for success. All along the way, expertise is needed instead of greed, purpose instead of multiples. If successful, there will be enough for everyone anyway. However, the right to a slice of the cake is acquired during the journey, not on the deckchairs behind the finish line.

The journey is sometimes arduous. Setbacks force you to pause, require a change of direction and often a completely new start. But this effort is worthwhile if the innovator succeeds in repeatedly reactivating the radiance of his innovation and the pulling power of his companions. Belief in one's own idea and the success of the innovation is the foundation on which all of this is based. It is the unshakeable DNA of innovation.

What it's all about

It's about your innovation, your vision, your ability to see things that are hidden from others. It is about your journey to success, about you and your belief in yourself and your abilities. It is about your awareness that the realisation of your innovation may be a long journey. And it's about maintaining the necessary naivety along the way that prevents you from recognising all the hurdles too far in advance. Because these hurdles can really spoil your enjoyment of the realisation. It's about regularly reassuring yourself that your innovation is something very special and that it's worth making the effort to realise it. It's about celebrating and enjoying the successes at each stage and allowing yourself to have fun on the journey again and again. A journey that is only fun at the end is not a journey to remember.

Deal with challenges creatively and openly. Deal with your companions openly and respectfully. Be and remain aware that it is you who will have to make unpleasant decisions when in doubt, who will take the rap if something goes wrong. Be and remain open to the concerns, needs and sensitivities of your companions, because they make the difference for you and your innovation. Recognise their skills and appreciate their commitment. All of this will help you get measurably closer to successfully realising your innovation every day – even if things don't go so well.

Who, if not you, should keep an eye on the goal so that your vision becomes the future. A future based on your innovation. A future for the good of the world. The success of your innovation will feel as overwhelming as the beating heart after the first transplant. Be courageous and go your own way. I wish you the right companions, the necessary resources and the right instinct for the requirements of your innovation at all times. It is worth it!

ABOUT THE AUTHOR

Dr. rer. pol. Sebastian Heinz, MSSc Human Geography, is a founding member of High Performance Battery Technology GmbH and High Performance Battery Holding AG, which he has headed up as Managing Director and CEO since July 2023.

Previously, he was responsible for the Internet of Things (IoT) in business customer sales at Telekom Deutschland.

With his dissertation on market development in the co-operation model, he developed an alternative strategy for the voluntary introduction of smart metering systems in Germany. The approaches developed therein are also suitable for the use of battery storage systems and thus open up the potential of platform models for the energy industry.

In 2018, he also founded the Institute for Innovation and Cooperation Management (InCoom), which specialises in the development of sustainable business models.

(OWN)ADVERTISING/ PUBLICITY/ INCREASE IN SALES

HPB | High Performance Battery Technology GmbH
highperformancebattery.de

HPB | LinkedIn
linkedin.com/company/ high-performance-battery-holding-ag

Dr. Sebastian Heinz | LinkedIn
linkedin.com/in/ sebastian-heinz-612199/

Dissertation
urn:nbn:de:hbz: 464-20170406-092750-1

Twinprint Publishing House
twinprint-verlag.de/ verlagsprogramm